ASPECTS OF HUDDERSFIELD 2

ASPECTS OF
HUDDERSFIELD
Discovering Local History 2

Edited by
Stephen Wade

Series Editor
Brian Elliott

Wharncliffe Books

First Published in 2002 by
Wharncliffe Books
an imprint of
**Pen and Sword Books Limited,
47 Church Street, Barnsley,
South Yorkshire. S70 2AS**

Copyright © Wharncliffe Books 2002

*For up-to-date information on other titles produced under the
Wharncliffe imprint, please telephone or write to:*

> **Wharncliffe Books
> FREEPOST
> 47 Church Street
> Barnsley
> South Yorkshire S70 2BR
> Telephone (24 hours): 01226 - 734555**

ISBN: 1-903425-23-9

A CIP catalogue record of this book is available from the
British Library

Cover illustration: *Market Square, Huddersfield, c.1910*

Printed in the United Kingdom by
CPI UK

CONTENTS

Market Square, *c.* 1910

INTRODUCTION

by

Stephen Wade

Readers of the *Aspects* series will be familiar with the charms of the eclectic nature of the subjects and range of material represented in the volumes. This book is no different from that, and follows closely the pattern set by Isobel Schofield, editor of *Aspects of Huddersfield 1*, and to whom I owe my thanks, as she did some of the gathering of essays for me here.

This pleasure in discovering fascinating fragments of social history through sheer serendipity is one of the principal reasons why local history has really taken off in recent years. The present volume supports that view, with a spectrum of topics extending from professional football to industrial history. Personally, I have always seen history as being a staggering assemblage of mosaics, making a massive, colourful pattern of meanings about the human experience. My contributors certainly present some intriguing and informative pieces in this specific little mosaic within the greater one.

Two writers, Ian Harlow and Robert Preedy, have concentrated on local cinema history, one from a practical viewpoint and one with a rather more acute eye for the commercial and the audience experience. Also in terms of recreation and leisure, we have Richard Stakes's celebration of the 'greats' of Huddersfield Town Football Club, whose story is an essential part of the town's sense of identity, of course, and deserves such a tribute.

Then we have the central focus of the book, the exploration of communities within the area as a whole, and here Vivien Teasdale, Alan J Brooke and myself take clearly identified groups and search for their significance. My own explorations revealed a 'forgotten people' with a European dimension, but this has been no less enlightening than the two more tightly-defined subjects.

Inevitably, any collection of pieces ranging across an area will come up with notable individuals, and Huddersfield has never been short of self-made men and creative people. John Oldham, Robert Gartery and Ian Sargen tell tales of people and families caught up in the macrocosmic forces of history, but give us a narrative standpoint firmly rooted in the plain experience of the individual caught up in the processes of power and historical change. In addition, John Goodchild's 'Sir Thomas Brooke' and David Griffiths's 'Read Holliday' bear witness to the achievements of remarkable men in periods of noted boom and expansion in those industries and enterprises inextricably linked with the Huddersfield area.

I would like to thank those who allowed interview time and helped with gaining access to the indispensable materials on which these essays are so reliant. In particular, Brian Haigh, Community History Manager of Kirklees MC Community History Service, Steve Carter, Anna Benbow, Stan Frontszak, Helen Roberts, Jan Tyminski and staff at West Yorkshire Archives deserve special thanks. Also, the series editor, Brian Elliott, has of course been very helpful.

I hope that these pieces play a part in the revisiting of places in that 'foreign country' of the past which never ceases to attract us.

1. THE HUDDERSFIELD LUDDITE REBELLION OF 1812

by John A Oldham

GEORGE MELLOR, ALIAS KING LUDD in the Huddersfield area, was hanged at York in January 1813, aged twenty-three, for his part in the Rebellion. This is the story of the Campaign he led.

The Luddite Rebellion started in Nottingham in 1811 and quickly spread to the North. The Huddersfield Campaign of 1812 merely lasted for about six months, yet it was one of the most violent and ferociously fought campaigns in the Luddite Rebellion. It centred on Huddersfield, including two local valleys carved out by the Colne and Spen rivers.

George Mellor was baptised in 1789, the same year as the French Revolution. The American Declaration of Independence had been made thirteen years earlier. King George III and his Government looked anxiously over their shoulders at France. England was a nervous and violent place and George grew up in a climate of fear and change.

George was born into an age of Revolution and Violence. The Huddersfield Luddite Campaign merely lasted for about six months, yet it was one of the most violent and ferociously fought campaigns in the Luddite Rebellion.

George's trade was cropping. It was their job to 'finish' a piece of cloth and make it fit for sale. The croppers converted rough woven cloth into an attractive piece of fabric. They added a great deal of value to the material and made sure they were going to get their fair share. This is why they were one of the best-paid groups of workers in the textile industry. The croppers had always jealously protected their industry through many years by means of their strong organisation. They were desperate to maintain laws, some of them going back to Elizabeth I, that had protected them from the threats of new inventions and unskilled people entering the trade. At the start of the nineteenth century they had collected the huge sum of ten thousand pounds. They used it to argue their case unsuccessfully before a Parliamentary Commission. Like Samson, the croppers had lost their strength. They were impotent to stop Parliament changing these laws.

So the croppers become powerless to stop the millowners installing new technology. Unskilled jobs were being created at the expense of thousands of croppers losing their jobs and businesses. The poet Blake captured the mood of many people when he wrote about the *Dark Satanic Mills*. Their world had been turned upside down and their trade was under threat.

They also believed that insult was added to injury when they were not allowed to gather together to discuss their plight. It is ironic that the accepted image of a Luddite is that of a vandal. It is not generally appreciated that they were fighting to save their jobs by having existing laws upheld. This is the reason why croppers became the main core of the Luddites in the West Riding. Eventually the croppers believed that they had exhausted all legal means to put their case, and felt compelled and justified to take direct action.

George's father had died when he was quite young and his mother had married John Wood, a Master Cropper. He educated George and gave him a trade. John Wood was considered a shadowy figure in Luddite history, and it is not known how much he 'used' George to save his own business. In 1811, at the time of the first Luddite Raids in Nottingham, George had not been long out of his apprenticeship.

It is difficult for us to appreciate that a working man, in the early nineteenth century, who could read and write, would have been under suspicion from the authorities. Literacy was a powerful tool in their hands. It helped to maintain their control and power over working people. If you were both a natural leader and literate, like George, you were considered dangerous. Because of this he quickly became a marked man.

The new shearing frames could finish much more cloth at a far cheaper price by cutting out the expensive hand cropping process.

Figure 1. The cloth fibres were cut (cropped) with huge shears that could weigh more than half a hundredweight. Croppers used them with the precision of a surgeon. This operation gave the woollen material a smooth finish. The work was both physically demanding and extremely skilful. A cropper could so easily ruin a piece of cloth.

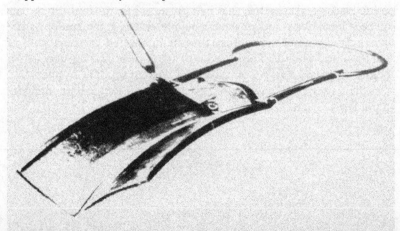

Figure 2. It was this invention over which the bloodiest Luddite uprising was fought in the West Riding. This Shearing Frame may look a Heath Robinson device, yet at a stroke it posed the greatest threat that this elite group of workers had ever faced. A piece of cloth was passed beneath two pairs of shearing shears. A simple gearing system opened and closed the shears. It took hardly any skill to operate and speeded up the cropping process considerably.

It is not difficult to see why the owners of the early textile mills wanted to install these shearing frames. The response of the Croppers and other workers to these new methods was swift and predictable.

George most likely read reports of the Nottingham Luddites to his work mates on a Saturday afternoon in their cropping shop. The first Luddite raids formed a model for the West Riding Luddites to follow. There were soon reports of Luddites drilling up the Colne Valley area of Huddersfield. Regular Luddite meetings were being held at the *Shears* pub in the Spen Valley and the *Crispin* at Halifax. Due to his literacy and physically commanding presence, George swiftly established himself as leader of the local Luddites and became King Ludd. He began to make preparations to follow the course taken by the Nottingham Luddites.

In February 1812 one of the earliest attacks of the Rebellion in the Huddersfield area was carried out in quite a spectacular fashion. A millowner in the Spen Valley, William Cartright, had ordered some shearing frames from The Taylor brothers at Marsden. Whilst the frames were carried across Hartshead Moor under the cover of darkness, the carriers were overcome and trussed up. The carriers

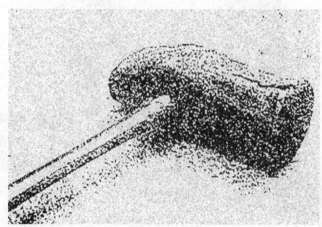

Figure 3. One of the Taylor brothers, who manufactured shearing frames, was called Enoch. The large hammer that the Luddites used to smash the frames was also called 'Enoch'. This gave rise to the Luddite saying 'Enoch shall make them and Enoch shall break them.'

were left at the side of the road, and the frames smashed. It was an outstanding success. Charlotte Bronte used this attack in her Luddite novel, *Shirley*. More raids followed on smaller shearing shops that had installed the frames.

The installation of the new shearing frames quickly started to have an impact on the croppers' trade. Exports had been banned to Napoleonic Europe, so there was a trade slump. The harvest had been poor and food prices were rising. Less work passed through the cropping shops, as more of it found its way into the mills to be completed by unskilled labourers using the new shearing frames. As the situation deteriorated some workers and their families were near starvation.

George persevered with small raids throughout February 1811. Yet he knew that he had to force the larger millowners to stop installing the shearing frames. The two local millowners in the area that had installed these frames were William Cartright in the Spen Valley and William Horsfall of Marsden. Horsfall was hated because of his statement, he would ride up to his saddle girth in Luddite blood if that was what was required to protect himself and his right to install the frames. Cartright had obviously not been deterred by their attack on his first shipment of frames.

The Luddites needed one big show of strength, so George started to devise an audacious plan. They had to take on and beat one of the largest millowners in the area.

Which one were they going to attack? It is said that matters were brought to a head with the toss of a coin at a secret meeting of the Luddites at the *Crispin Inn*. Legend has it that only George saw the coin. Nevertheless, the momentous decision was taken to press home their case, with the largest attack they had ever mounted, on Cartright's' mill.

On a cold night in April 1812, Luddites started to assemble in a field next to the *Dumb Steeple* for the attack on Rawfolds Mill. The

Figure 4. The *Dumb Steeple* was the meeting point for the attack on Rawfolds Mill that was intended to put the balance of power back into the hands of the Luddites.

steeple was just below Kirklees Hall, Huddersfield's claim as the final burial place of Robin Hood. George had expected four hundred to turn up. In the event about half that number came to support him.

For the attack on Rawfolds Mill, George insisted that everyone wore a hat to avoid suspicion. Disguises of masks and womens' clothes would be abandoned after the attack.

And rum had been brought to lift the spirits. George gave the order for everyone to be put into ranks and numbered off. Near eleven o' clock the army of Luddites silently started their march over to the Spen Valley. *Rawfolds Mill* was approximately three miles away, and the first part of their walk took them up the hill to the village of Hartshead. They passed *Thorn Bush Farm,* where the new incumbent at the church, Reverend Patrick Bronte, was trying to sleep. It is highly likely that the clergyman passed on the story of the Luddite army marching past his lodgings to Charlotte. He was so concerned for his safety that afterwards he purchased a pistol to defend himself. The parishioners of Howarth have the Luddites to thank for their vicar discharging a weapon every morning from the rectory steps!

In Charlotte Bronte's Luddite novel *Shirley* William Cartright, the owner of Rawfolds mill, is portrayed in quite a romantic way with French family connections. In reality he was a successful millowner who had outstanding qualities of toughness and resilience. He had no hesitation in taking on the Luddites when he saw they were trying to stifle the development of his business. Cartright had already suffered one attack on his shearing frames and was determined to defend his mill at all costs. Soldiers were stationed and slept in the mill. Large flagstones could be quickly hoisted behind windows to provide cover, and a bell was installed to summon help for more soldiers, should it be required.

The march up the hill to Hartshead and down to Rawfolds Mill in the Spen Valley appeared to pass without incident. Many more local people other than Reverend Patrick Bronte would have heard the tramping feet of the army of Luddites as they passed. None would have raised the alarm. The Luddites operated and survived with the tacit support of the community. The silence of most of the people in their community was a powerful weapon in their campaign.

Cartright was ready for a Luddite attack. Spiked rollers were positioned at the top of stairways and containers of acid were ready to be poured on any Luddites who managed to get into the mill.

As the small army approached the Spen Valley from the south, they were hoping for a contingency from Leeds to be moving towards them from the north. George had been promised support so that two armies would converge on Rawfolds Mill. He halted his men on the hillside above the mill and waited. A signal never came from the north of the valley. George obviously deliberated and finally decided that he would risk the attack with his own men.

The attack had been carefully rehearsed. The hammer men went in first, with cover provided by the musket men. Guards that Cartright had positioned outside the mill were quickly overcome. It was the barking of a dog that sounded the alarm. The response from Cartright to the first splinters of wood from the hammer men on his doors, and the sound of muskets and broken glass, was decisive. He also had rehearsed his plan. Someone was dispatched immediately to the bell to toll for extra help from the military further down the valley. He woke the soldiers and started firing down into the mill yard where scores of screaming Luddites had now swarmed in.

In hindsight it's easy to understand why the attack failed against such well-organised and stiff opposition. Although the Luddites had the advantage of surprise, they were literally sitting ducks in the mill yard. There was no cover for them whatsoever from the volleys of gunfire that rained down and killed at least two of them.

George had counted on victory at the Battle of Rawfolds to shift the balance of power back in favour of the West Riding Luddites. It was quite a close run thing, but it was the first and most spectacular defeat of the Luddites. The effect on the future course of Luddism in the West Riding was devastating.

The Luddite defeat at the Battle of Rawfolds Mill was a devastating blow to their campaign.

After the defeat at Rawfolds, George must have felt victory in the campaign slipping away from him, so he resorted to desperate measures. If he couldn't attack the mills, he would attack the millowners.

Immediately after the battle of Rawfolds an unsuccessful attempt was made to shoot Cartright. This assassination attempt signalled a new twist in George's tactics.

A few weeks later William Horsfall was returning from market day in Huddersfield. Having crossed Longroyd Bridge, near to John Wood's cropping shop, his journey took him westward up the Colne Valley. He stopped at the Warren House for refreshment. A few hundred yards beyond the public house was a plantation where three figures were waiting for him. At the Special Commission in York the prosecution would successfully argue that George was one of these.

Horsfall continued his journey after his stop at the public house. A traveller who followed closely behind him heard shots and raced his horse up to Horsfall, whom he found slumped at the saddle. He was taken back to the Warren House and a surgeon was called. The victim was never moved from the public house and died later from his wounds.

After Horsfall's murder the Luddites began to lose sympathy with their local community, who had protected and supported them during their campaign. Attacking mills was one thing. Killing millowners was another. Although many threats had been made against Horsfall, Cartright and the local magistrate Radcliffe, this was the first time that someone had suffered fatally at the hands of the Luddites.

The murder sent shock waves through county and country. It played into the hands of Joseph Radcliffe, because it forced the government to finally grant his constant requests for more troops. Eventually there were more troops in the Luddite Campaign under the 'Commander of the North', General Maitland, than were committed to Wellington in the Peninsular Wars. The authorities were careful never to actually declare martial law, but the woollen towns of the West Riding to all intents and purposes become garrisons.

Horsfall's murder sent shock waves through county and country.

The outrage that followed Horsfall's murder galvanised public opinion to demand that 'something had to be done.' Thus began a tale of intrigue, spies, *agents provocateurs* and torture that would put down the Rebellion with such brutal force. Over the next few months the Luddites must have reckoned that the gods themselves had served notice against their campaign. In their desperation, the government turned to a military genius and diplomat to quell the Luddite Rebellion, General Maitland.

About the same time as Horsfall's murder, Maitland was heading a military convoy that stretched over twelve miles into Manchester. The reign of fear by 'King Tom' had begun in the North.

Maitland was shrewd and determined to succeed where others had failed. Before he marched over the Pennines into Yorkshire he put together a formidable team. This small and select group included Captain Raynes who used maverick tactics to get results. Maitland backed him, against the advice of other officers, and formed what was considered the first commando style unit in the army. John Lloyd, the clerk to Stockport's magistrate, also joined the team. He had a gift for gathering vital intelligence. His methods would include physical and mental torture in order to get a result.

The appointment of General Maitland as Commander in the North signalled a determination by the government to finally crush the Luddite Rebellion through brutal means, including torture.

Maitland gathered intelligence himself in the North West. He came to believe, contrary to the panic in London and the Government, that this Rebellion did not have the vast support of the people. Northern England was not about to explode into a fire of republicanism. Many of the causes were obvious. People were near starvation, wages were dropping and food prices were soaring.

Maitland surmised, therefore, that he had to try to contain the violence. He needed to buy time to allow the trade position to improve and help to change the climate of public opinion. He knew that in the short term, however, that some tough measures would be needed.

Having assembled his team and perfected their methods Maitland turned his attention to Yorkshire in the late summer of 1812. Captain Raynes and Lloyd started their intelligence gathering that would eventually lead to arrests. They also brought with them their brutal methods, including torture, that would put fear into the heart of the communities of Huddersfield.

George was repeatedly brought before the local magistrate at Minsbridge House and released for lack of evidence.

As the authorities started to get the upper hand, General Maitland started to give some thought as to how to bring the government Campaign to an effective conclusion. He needed something that would provide retribution against the Luddite leaders and their followers. It was necessary that it would be administered in such a way that everyone could see it and no one would ever forget it. The solution was to hold a form of show trial at York called the 'Special Commission'.

The outcome of the Special Commission was considered so important that there is evidence that in December 1812, prior to the Commission opening in January 1812, General Maitland discussed the penalties to be given to George and his co-defendants. Any chance of a martyr's burial was ruled out through a prior agreement to anatomise their bodes.

By October 1812 George was the leader of a Rebellion that was effectively over. He was sent for trial to the Special Commission at York on the evidence of two apprentices employed by his cousin, John Mellor. Local legend has it that as George mounted the stage coach on Leeds Road he tried, without success, to generate a final cheer from the crowd of disillusioned people who had gathered to see his departure. George's reputation had fallen to such a low ebb as people began to realise that the dream offered by the croppers would never be realised.

General Maitland decided to finally crush the Rebellion by having a show trial at York. The sentences would be so brutal that they would teach the Luddites and their followers a lesson they would never forget.

By the end of 1812 over one hundred Luddite leaders and their sympathisers had been incarcerated at York castle prison awaiting trial. The prison was so over-crowded that the governor feared a break out.

There was considerable public interest in the trials at York. The stream of traffic on the Huddersfield to York road had swelled after the Christmas break. The editor of the *Leeds Mercury* had even planned to publish a special supplement.

Crucial to the success of the Special Commission was the appointment of the judges. Lessons had been learned from the Nottingham trials. The 'leniency' shown by Judge Bayley had, the authorities believed, given the wrong signals to George and others to feel that they too could get away without punishment. So Judge Bayley was ruled out and two 'hard liners' brought in, Judges Thompson and Le Blanc.

The first trial of the Special Commission opened on Monday .... January 1813. It was not the show trial of George and his friends for Horsfall's murder the authorities wanted. Their counsel had gained a delay until Wednesday.

A large crowd had gathered long in the early hours of Wednesday morning, long before George's trial was due to be heard. Edward Baines, editor of the *Leeds Mercury* recorded the excitement generated by this trial, '....has seldom been equalled in a court of justice.'

George was finally brought into the dock in chains to a packed courthouse. He was accused with his friend William Thorpe, and workmate Thomas Smith, of the murder of William Horsfall.

'...You have been sworn into a question of blood.'

Thus the government attorney, Park, opened his case with these

chilling words. They were spoken by a man who knew he already had
a result before the trial started. He started as he meant to proceed
throughout this trial, using quite unscrupulous methods under the
eyes of a judge who was more than willing to make those eyes blind.
The first set of witnesses merely added gore to Park's description.

**'...You have been sworn into a question of blood.' These
chilling words were from the opening statement of the
Government attorney ...spoken by a man who knew he
already had a result before the trial started... .**

Park now called his chief witness, Ben Walker. He was a work
colleague of George and had been accused, together with George
and his friends, of Horsfall's murder. Walker had turned King's
Evidence. George's attorney, Brougham, never even bothered to
cross-examine this key prosecution witness and left it to his junior.
The accused had considered themselves lucky that they had secured
Brougham as their counsel. Throughout the trial they placed their
total trust in him. It is possible, through reading the transcript of the
trial, to reach the conclusion that Brougham had given up on this
case, because he hardly spoke in the trial. He may have considered it
a lost cause with such a weakly prepared defence and such strong
evidence.

The defence case was largely based on alibis. Sadly George had
pinned his faith in a line of defence that was to be effectively scorned
at by the judge. In his summing up he sarcastically commented 'how
was it that so many good people of Yorkshire could remember so
accurately the time of these most ordinary events in the street and in
the workshop after an interval of six months.'

The jury left the court to consider their verdict at 7.55 pm.
Twenty-five minutes later they returned. The editor of the *Leeds
Mercury*, Edward Baines, recorded the eerie silence that passed over
the court. He noted the stillness that was broken when the foreman
announced the verdict of 'Guilty.' He remarked on the dignity and
self-composure shown by the three accused.

Judge LeBlanc decided to waste no time when he ordered the
execution to be carried out in just over twenty-four hours time, on
Friday morning. The show trial was going to produce the
execution of George and his colleagues that Maitland so
desperately wanted to help finally put down the rebellion.

**There was going to be no chance of appeal or deferral of
sentence. As Judge LeBlanc put on the black cap he told the
men to, '...make the best use you can of the period still
allotted to you'. They were to be, '...severally hanged by the**

neck until they were dead'.

Friday was recorded as being cold and fine. Maitland wanted to extract the maximum amount of publicity from these first executions. He was risking nothing as regards security. Every avenue had been sealed off and guarded by ranks of infantry. The Cavalry was waiting in case of any trouble and two troops of dragoons were lined up in front of the gallows to thwart any last minute escape attempt. Just before 9 am, under the shadows of the prison walls, the Judges and Jury and those who had taken part in the trial assembled.

A new type of scaffold had been erected for the Special Commission. Several prisoners could be executed at the same time. General Maitland wanted a 'show execution' to reveal the whole body after the drop, rather than just head and feet.

The three men were led in chains, from the castle prison up to the scaffold. The chaplain invited them to pray and they went down on their knees. George confessed his sins, but not to the crime. He asked for his enemies, who may be present, to be forgiven and his prayer is recorded as having had a profound melancholic effect on the crowd. If Maitland had planned a show execution, so had George. He remained on his knees for ten minutes, far longer than the other two. He spoke passionately as he made sure his last message was heard.

After the execution, their bodies were taken away immediately to York General Hospital. They were dissected and anatomised under a military guard. It is recorded that the Government Solicitor walked the streets of York immediately after the executions. He recorded the defeat and broken spirits in the faces of the 'adherents of the prisoners in York'.

The Special Commission petered out in the early part of the second week. It had achieved exactly the result that Maitland had planned. He was not the sort of man to see lives taken unnecessarily. The politician in him was looking to the future rebuilding of the shattered trust between the local communities and the authorities.

Even if we make allowances for the difference between the legal standards of Georgian Britain and our own, it was clear that the Luddites were never going to get a fair hearing. The establishment had agreed on the results of some of the more important trials before the Commission had started. The threat of the Luddites to the country was considered so great by the authorities that the outcome was a foregone conclusion. Under the cloak of the rule of law, the Luddites and their community suffered one of the most appalling acts of violence and brutality perperpetrated by the UK Government.

It was clear that the Luddites were never going to get a fair hearing.

Maitland's analysis had been right. Things started to improve with Napoleon's defeat in Russia and the lifting of the ban on exports. A better harvest helped to bring down prices and trade improved. It is bitterly ironic that this would have been achieved without the Luddite Rebellion.

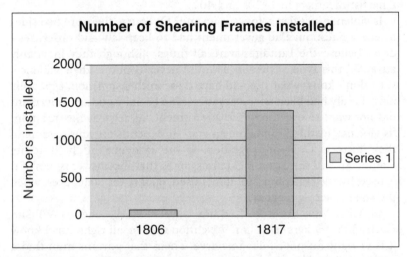

Figures 5a & 5b. The effect on the cropping trade was a total disaster. These statistics speak for themselves. Only 100 cropping frames had been installed by 1806. This had risen to 1,462 frames by 1817. In the same year, of 3,625 croppers who petitioned parliament, only 860 were in full time work.

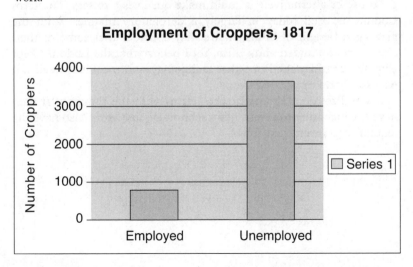

The plight of the croppers was now dire. Emigration was an answer for some. Yet existing laws prevented taking the skills of our most important trade abroad. Lord Lascelles made a plea to the Home Secretary, Lord Sidmouth, to amend legislation and give financial assistance for relocation. Sidmouth consulted the Prime Minister, Lord Liverpool, who refused.

Some emigrated, despite the restrictions, rather than live with the fear of further reprisals. There were stories that the men who took part in the battle of Rawfolds which were said to have re-emerged at Chartist meetings in 1830s and 40s.

Is violence justified to pursue an end? Of course there are two sides to every question. The government had to keep law and order. Yet I don't believe the Luddites were all thugs, although they inevitably attracted this type of person. I would never condone their violence, yet I don't know what I would have done in their position, especially if my family had been near starvation. The broad Luddites movement did not want to overthrow the government. As regards the question: 'is violence justified to pursue an end?' it depends on your reading of their history. One interpretation of the evidence of the Luddite Campaign and the Special Commission is that the answer is 'yes' if it is used by the state, but 'no' if it is used against the state, even when the state is acting illegally.

In Charlotte Bronte's Luddite novel *Shirley*, one of William Cartright's workers tells him, 'Invention may be all right, but I know it isn't right for poor folks to starve. Them that governs mun find a way to help us.'

The quest for new technology is insatiable. It is inevitable that new inventions will be continually made and they cannot be 'un-invented'. Technology is a double-edged sword that can be put to good use or alternatively it could make our lives a misery. The term Luddite is used today in largely a derogatory manner. With the privileged benefit of hindsight we may consider that some of their aims were misguided and selfish. Yet I believe that the Luddites kept alive for us today the hope that technology and machines need not necessarily dominate our lives.

It was President Kennedy who left us with the thought, 'If men have the ingenuity to invent new technology, they must also have the ingenuity to invent new jobs.'

2. JAMES HIRST OF POLE MOOR: 'BOOK APRIL 24TH, 1836 NOTABLE THINGS OF VARIOUS SUBJECTS IN DIARY FORM'

by Robert Gartery

JAMES HIRST LIVED FROM 1813-1901 (Figures 1 & 2) in the family cottage at Wortshill, Pole Moor, Slaithwaite. His diary is now in the West Yorkshire Archives in Wakefield and contains many items of interest. Where possible James Hirst's own spelling and punctuation have been retained.

Figure 1. James Hirst, aged 80, and his sister, in 1893.

Figure 2. James Hirst working at his loom at home in 1890.

The first section includes many recipes for everyday problems and the curing of illnesses – one wonders if the patient survived the cure!

>   The juice of groundling¹ snuft up into the nose out of a spoon or saucer purgeth the head marvellously and it takes away the greatest and oldest pain thereof that is, this medicine is worth gold though it be very cheap I have known them that have had marvellous pains in the head almost intolerable for the space of a dozen years and this helped them presently and have never had pain since they took this medicine.
>
>   Dry the roots of red nettles and make them powder and drink a spoonful of the powder thereof in a draught of white wine some thing warm and it will break the stones² though it be never so great and that with the speed use it every day and the gravel be all broken and consumed. A thing of small price and grat virtue.
>
>   Let the party that bleedeth chew the root of a nettle in his mouth but swallow it not down and without doubt the blood will staunch for if one keep it in his mouth he can loose no more blood – Petrus Hispanuch.
>
>   Recipe for destroying catterpillers on gosebery tree. Take a large basket full of Elder leaves boil them in as much water as will cover them till the liquor becomes quite black (which will require three or four hours) then clear and cool it and to every two gallons of liquor add one gallon of Tobacco water lay it on the trees with a fine water

can when they are quite dry and in ten minutes the catterpillers will fall off taken from the Leeds Mercury *of Saturday July 18th 1836.*

The dung of a cat dried and mixed with strong vinegar, that it may be something thick, and there with any Hairy place rubbed oftentimes or anointed in the day, it will cause that Hair to grow no more in that place – Proved by a countryman saith Mizaldous.

Pottage made of the leaves and roots of strawberries being eaten fasting certain days, of them that have the Jaundice, doth help them perfectly – this was the secret of a certain Monk wherewith he got marvelous much money.

Cast brimstone³ into a chafing dish with hot burning coals, and hold a red rose over the smoke thereof and it will be white.

Earthworms slit and cleansed and washed from their slime and earthy matter (half a dozen of them) and cut in pieces or chopped and a good mess of pottage made thereof, made with oatmeal and water, and so much every day eaten by them that have black Jaundice, for the space of twelve days or longer, no doubt it will perfectly cure them thereof, though it be never so long, and rooted and though it be past cure, or else a spoonful of the powder of them made in March or any other time when you can catch them taken every day so long in a little draught of any drink doeth perfectly cure the same – This is very true and hath oftentimes proved it hath some in four or five days.

This following is a true and proved medicine for the Tooth ache. Take a handful of ground Ivy and much Spearmint and as much salt. Stamp them a little together then put all the same into a pint of vinigar and seeth all well over the fire then strain it well and put the same into a close glassen vessel or bottle and when you will use it take a spoonfull thereof and put it onto the side of the mouth that acheth and hold down your cheek that it may desend to the roots of the Aching Teeth and it will take the Ach and pain away presently – this was taught me by a woman to whom many resorted for help who only used this medicine therefor.

An egg laid on a Thursday and emptied and filled with salt and set in the fire remaining there until it may be made into powder and the cankered Teeth rubbed with the powder thereof it both kills the canker and the worms that eat the Teeth and destroys them – proved.

Quick lime mixed with old cheese and well beaten together will fasten and glue strongly together broken stone vessels and also broken glass – This was credibly told me for a great secret by one that proved it.

Grind mustard with vinegar and rub it hard and well into the Palms of the hands or soles of the feet and it will help and quicken forgetful persons – Petrus Hispanus.

Whosoever eateth two walnuts two figs twenty leaves of rue and one grain of salt all stamped and mixed together fasting shall be safe from Poison or plage that day which antidote King Mithridas had used so much that when he drank poison deliberately to kill himself it would not hurt him.

If you mark where your right foot doth stand at the first time you hear the Cuckoo, and then grave or take up the earth under the same wheresoever the same is sprinkled about there will be no fleas breed – I have known it proved true.

To make an excellent eyewash take one penny worth of the flower of Zink and one pennyworth of white coproise and about the bigness of a peg of Blue vitrel mix them up together in a Quart of Spring water – this has been often proved.

Cure for Hydrophobia[4]

A correspondent thus writes to the Morning Herald – You lately published several letters about this frightful disease and I find on looking over an old Book published in 1760 that the following is contained therein – Take the leaves of rue picked from the stalks and bruised venice treacle or mithridate and the scrapings of pewter of each of four ounce. Boil all these over a slow fire in two quarts of strong ale till one pint is consumed then keep it in bottles close stopped and give it nine spoonfulls to a man or woman seven morning together with fasting and six to a dog. This must be followed out within nine days from the bite. Apply some of the ingredients to the bitten places this reciept was take out of Cathorp Church in Lincolnshire the whole town being bitten by a mad dog and all that took this medicen did well and the rest died mad.

Taken from the *Yorkshire Post*, 28 July 1866

The second section contains a 'count of old ancient particulares' covering many events between 1795 and 1890. His main interests seem to have been the price of oatmeal, wheat and flour and the variations in the weather – especially the snows and floods that seem to have been a hazard of the time. A selection has been made of the more interesting entries. In 1799 the conditions seem to have been very hard.

July 25 1795 Oat meal Sold at £0s 15 0d per Hoop.

Feby 1799 A very deep snow & another at Easter a very late cold Spring Suceeded & also a very cold and rainy summer and Autum.

17 Augt 1799 A very heavy flood which Swept away the Corn Mill Dam the old chapel yard Two houses at the Bridge and in Lingards, and did great damage to corn and Hay, and a very dear time suceeded.

18 August 1799 the Reservoy Frightened many of the Housholders from their Habitations.

30 August 1799 Another great flood which Did much damage to the canals and the corn Mill dam broke again.

22 Sept 1799 Another great flood which broke the wair in the old Chapel yard a Second time and did much damage, this was said to be the heavest flood in many places of the country a greavous time Suceeded.

2 Dec 1799 Meal very bad s13 0d per hoop, Weat flour old s16 0d per hoop.

Jany 1 1800 Deep snow. Meal at s14 0d per Hoop.

Wages for Spinning white wool 20oz or 1lb for 1d.

Septr 21 1821 avery great flood which did much Damage took one house at kitchen part of Mill mery Dale broke up Tyse Lane also Rishworth Mill swept away one Mill and dyehouse in Holmfirth John Sykes Black Smith two fields to mow in

1826 Dobson Bank broke and Several more which caused great distress in many parts of England and work was very scarce so that people went a Singing into different parts of the country this was very hot and drufty summer and there was light crops of grass 7 corn top of fould well was dry many weeks.

Feby 4 1831 there fell a very great Snow which was the eight of our door and there was a great drift in the back wass which was ier than the walls.

1836 there was a late Spring and grass and corn was very late the principal part of the Hay was to get August 1st. And there was a very cold wet autum and corn was very late and there fell a great Snow *October 28th & 29th* there was drifts three or four foot deep.

1837 there was a very hard winter there was some seveare frosts and the Spring was very late there set in a frost on the 11th March on the 26th there fell a great Snow & the frost continued from March 10th till April 15th & then there was alight shower of rain and it turned to snowing and freezing very ceenly again and there was some of the snow that fell on the 10th March to be seen on the 10th May on the tops of the ills.

1838 There was a very survare frost and a snow fell on January 2 which staid untill l February 7 and on that day there was a thaw and on Feby 9 there fell another snow and it began to feez again untill March 1 and then it thew again untill March 3 then turned to freezing again untill and it was a very cold and a very late Spring there was little or no rain untill the 21st of May and then it was a very wet Summer and tere was a very Bad hay time.

1839 January 7 there was a terable high wind which did a very great *deal of damage in almost every part of England blew down 11 steam chimnes at Blackburn and blew a very great deal of trees down in different parts of the country slates chimnes windows and church spires it blew one of the clock faces of Huddersfield church steeple and the lead of the top of the church.*

1841 There was a very hard winter and a very great deal of snow, so that the roads were snown up and the windows frozen from Feby 1 to 10th and never thawn. Blind Janney died Feby 24th aged 72 years.

1841 there was a very fine March, from 7th to 17th it was very warm and pleasant weather so that people had to doff their close it was so warm Leeds times Saturday March 26th the Weather during the past week the past weather has been warmer that it was ever known in the month of March by the oldest inhabitant of Huddersfield vegitation is progressing rapidly and it is also alleged that the Cuckoo has been frequently heard to sing in the neighbourhood during this winter and Spring there is disorder among Cows which affected their feet and mouths so that they could neither stand nor eat.

1846 there was a very mild fine January and February and it was not so fine in March it was frosty April was very wet till the 4th for 3 days and 3 nights it Snew and there was a very great Snow and coaches were driven fast in the deep cutting on Stanege black Billberys got in the wite lee Roof Nov 15th 1846 coming from Deanhead Chapel The disorder in the Potatoes was very bad again this year at Christmas they was selling at 1d per ld.

1852 February 4th dreadfull Calamity at Holmfirth by the Bursting of a Reservoir several Mill entirely destroyed and whole families Swept away. Upwarsds of one hundred lives lost and immense loss of property Digley Mill and factory and 7 houses Barn Dyehouse and several more buildings swept away.

1853 May 9th there was a very great Snow there was snow drifts as high as the walls the deep cutting on top of Stanige had to be schole the morning following before the carts could go & the Railway train from Sheffield to Huddersfield was stopped & had to stop on the line till morning it bgan to snow by 6 Oclock in the morning and continued till after 9 at night without intermission. Corn was very late and very dear this year. October 31 double Supper flour 11s 6d per Hoop Meal 8s 6d per Hoop Burnt Plats pooled down May 1853.

1857 August 14th There was a very great flood it began to rain at halfpast nine at night & thundered & lightened till betwix one & two in the morning it rained all the time & did a great deal of damage in different parts of the country bursting dams 7 taking bridges down.

*   I stood at Huddersfield Cloth Hall with Pieces Black & Steel*

Doeskin 17 years I began to stand in the Market first time in March 1847. And after I atended the Market Days till the year 1864. But I attended Huddersfield 32 years with respect to the piece buisness & the Shop Keeping buisness.

1860 There was a very frosty winter it was not more than 24 hours from Christmas to May 5 but it did free either more or less & a very late Spring it was & hay was very scarce & dear after May 5th it was very fine & pleasant till May 28th when there fell a snow which covered the ground with a very could boysterous east wind which did a great deal of damage in different parts of the country.

I have heard my Mother say that the year my Brother John was born there had never been no Snow at Old Christmas day and that the year was 1822.

1860 This was the coldest and wetest Summer in the recolection of any one living the hay was nearly all spoiled & the corn was very little good for but to be made into fodder for the cattal it did not yeld towards ripening till a frost came on the 12th of October which was so keen that we could not spread muck in the far Owler it was so frozen & this frost caused the corn to ripen very quickly afterwards.

1866 June 19th There was a darkness at one o'clock Noon it was dark as if it had been night & it lasted about half an hour. This was a very wet summer from July 25th to October 7th there was seldom a Day but it Rained either more or less & it was a very bad Corn time. There was a great flood November 16th which did cause a great deal of damage in Yorkshire & Lancashire 4 Persons drounded in Rishworth by crossing a wood Bridge & Deanhead Reservoyer Bank slipped & it was in great danger of bursting.

1868 there was a very forward Spring and a very drufty Summer most of the Springs was dry and the fields Burned. black Bilberys got on top of Wortshill. June 21 there was plenty of Coorn Shorn July 21st. And on July 28th there broke out a great fier on Slaithwaite & Marsden Moore it was supposed to Burn 1000 acres. The first Rain that came was on August 11th and on August 22nd but the heaviest Rain fell on September 25th.

1872 this was a Wet Summer and a Good deal of Thunder. July 13th There was a very great flood it rained hard for 6 hours and did a great deal of damage the destructive ravages of the great storm which passed over the North of England on Friday and Saturday were wide spread. Never probably within living memory has such a large amount of destruction been wrought within a short space of time in Lancashire the swoolen waters of the Irwell and its tributary at Medlock did imense amount of injury. Factories and dwelling houses

*were devastated and in several cases hunen life was lost between 50
and 60 Bodies washed out of their graves in Manchester. The potatoes
was very bad this year potatoes sold at 18d per stone.*

*The foot & mouth disease was very bad. An the rinderpes the year
1872 will be for ever memorable in the tables of rainfall there was
2278 days on which rain fell and 11 of snow thunder occurred on 29
days the total rainfall for the year was 4,020 tons to the acre.*

*Coal was very dear this year in March was 16d per 112lbs Slaithwaite
Coals And Lower Pit Coals in April 10.5 Load Cost 18s 6d Livered at
our house. There was a great Thunder storm on July 23rd No fewer
than 10 Persons were Killed by the Lightening Namely 1 at Leeds at
Branhope 1 at Shields 1 at Berwick 1 at Brompton near Northallerton
and 5 at Preston a number of Horses & cattle & sheep & houses.*

*1874 July 21. There was a dreadfull thunder storm it struck far
Wortshill Laith and Burnt it up with all the Crop of Hay on both Wm
Haigh & John Bamforth's Farm's the Ass was takeing shelter at
Laith end & was killed. Also at Owler Clough the Lightening struck
the Corbel on the Liath nook and then it went on down into the mistal
Joseph Bamforth was in the Mistal and was knocked down and it
killed a Hen & split the Muck fork shaft. Also at shayes Laith
scammonden it struck the Chimney and went down into the house
and bor Pictures glasses & furniture. Also the Electorick fluid stuck
George's Oshutt & Shuttlers.*

*1882 Severe Snowstorm on Wednesday December 6th a heavy fall of
snow took place over almost the whole of England and Wales and
Scotland and caused great delays in Railway traffic while in some
towns tramcar and omnibus traffic was entirely stopped. There as not
been such a snow since 1831. It snew all our Chamber windows up so
that I could not see to whave for two days and all the roads was made
up and had to be Shooled*

*1883 January 25 & 26 There was a very strong wind which dida
great deal of damage in different parts of the country up rooting trees
and blowing chimneys down. November 30 Was a very dark Day it
was almost as dark as Night at two o'clock in the afternoon and it
was so dark most of one hour and they could not see to Weave and it
was very dark all afternoon. December 6th Waterside Mill Burned
down and all the Machinary it was burned down once before in 1793*

*1886 January 28 The Last House at Burnt Plats destroyed. Jimmey
Pizord was Buried this day. Bill Gledhill of the Poor House wanted to
have the House when Pizord was dead and when he went to the
Stewards at Slaithwaite and got concent to have it he was to pool the
chimney of and make what use he likjed of it. But not a dwelling*

House. And he came and pooled the chimney of before the buring folk had got to Pole. I know Pizord had a great deal of company visited him at nights and on Sundays and that they had hamed to keep it as a resorting Place and they were so inraged that they came in at Night Pizord was buried and pooled the thack of and gathered all the woods together and the coals that there was and set it on fire this was the end of the last House at Burnt Plats.

1886 July 23 There was a great flood and thunder which did a great deal of damage it did a great deal of damage in Tyse lane and took Merrydale Bridge and the Bridge above graystone below Reapfield and a great deal of damage at clough House mill. And I never saw it come into our Parlour so in my life it came on the floor to under the Bed Stands and I had to be very bisey with the Besom sweeping down the back of the door els it wood have filled the House.

1887 June 20th Selebration of The Queens Jubilee on the top of Wortshill there was a Great fire composed of 4 tuns of coals and vast amounts of old sleepers that had come from the Railway and a hogshead of gass tar and maney gallon of Parrofen Oil. And there was never such a Fire on the top of Wortshill seen before. And there was many hundred Folks and there was many a one that staid with it all night.

1887 December John Hirst Ladcastle Saddleworth Library of Books was Sold by auction in London there was 3,476 of them and they sold for upwards of £3000

1888 Flour was the cheapest that I ever knew it from July 25th 1887 to September 7th 1888 Good Flower as ned to be eaten sold it 1s 8d per Stone of 16 lbs.

1888 November Powle Chapel Struck by Lightening and it knocked the Chimney of there was a thunder storm and it was so dark at half past eleven o clock that they could not see what clock it was by the arthstone

1895 June 26 there was a dreadful Thunder storm it began about 4 oclock in the afternoon. It did a great deal of damage in different parts of the country it continued almost 3 ours. It rained ailstones and frost lumps on the ground at Slaithwaite was wite the morning after and it killed a good many foolk in different parts of the country.

1895 July 19 Thunder boult fell at Goms o Land. And it did a deal of damage mashed most of the windos out and mashed through the thack and did a deal of damage up and down the house and Chamber. Set a bed on fire in the Chamber Luckey there was no one in the house at the time.

James Hirst also describes his visits to other parts of the area and further afield by foot, cart and on the newly built railways.

1836 May 24th It was Whitsun Tuesday I got up by 4 oclock in the morning. I had long had a great desire to see Manchester and I got up and set of and never aquainted none of our folks and I walked till I got to granes Bar then I took a cart and I got a ride into Manchester about 9 oclock and I lost no time in seeing what I could. I went to the Railway Station and saw the first Railway Carriages that I had ever seen in my life. I went to Cheethams13 Coledge the old Church the Exchange St Anns Square and all the notable places till about 3 oclock. I set off towards home again and walked all the way home and got back about 8 oclock.

1837 It was Ripponden feast Sunday I went my first time to Studley Pike with Sister Sarah and Brother Joseph. We set of about 10 oclock in the forenoon and we went through Rishworth up by Harry Bins factory and through Turven and a hard trudge we had of it we was all of us hungary and well tired before we got back home again. It is very bad travelling over the moores.

1852 May 31 I went to Liverpool & went to Black rock batorey saw Nelsons moneyment custom house exchange sailors home & many other fine buildings.

1854 July 17 I went on a cheap trip to Ripon Studley park and fountains habbey Ripon Minster & went on the top of the tower there are trees in Studley park 164 feet high the tower at fountains abbey is 166.5 feet high & a wonderful place it is.

1858 June 2nd I went to look at Beaumont Park. I went from Huddersfield by Lockwood and came back by Crossland Hill and down Pimroyde Cowersley lane and Smith Riding and over Low westwood and Wellhouse up Bank end Bolster moor and Clough head up Mellor lane by the Ratten up the Hard home. I got home by 8 oclock.

1858 September 19th I went on A Pleasure Excursion at 10 oclock in the forenoon & did not rest above one hour till eleven o clock at Night from Wortshill to Crofthouse from Crofthouse to Firth house Mill from Firth house Mill to Ripponden Slack from Rippponden Slack to Butterworth from Butterworth to Tryangle from Tryangle to Sorby from Sorby to Luddenden foot from Luddenden foot to Mytholm Royd from Mytholm Royd to Studley Pike from Studley Pike to Whiteholme Reservoy from Whiteholm Reservoy to turven Road from Turven Road to Blackstone Edge from Blackstone Edge to Batings from Batings to Pike end in Rishworth from Pike end to Cunning corner from Cunning corner to Moselden gate from Moselden gate to Broad Lee from Broad Lee to Wortshill.

1860 July 15th I went to Mr John Hirts's Dobcross Saddleworth it was on a Sunday and I went to Mr John Hirst Junr & his two Daughters to Dobcross Church in the Fornoon and in the afternoon I

went with Mr John Hirst to their new Mill called Bank field Mill.
And then we went to his fathers at Grove house Delph and got
drinking then I came back by train to Slaithwaite Station.

1863 August 2 it was Sunday. I went to Halifax with Wm Haigh far
wortshill we set off from home at 1 oclock and we went by Stainland
went on to Beecon hill and to the Peoples Park and the orphanage
Scircoat and came back by Meatley Bottom and Butterworth and
Steel Lane and Hey Lane and got home by 9 oclock at Night. Halifax
was greatly decorated on account of the Prince and Princess of Wales
coming to visit it on the folowing day.

1874 August 26 I had a Grand trip to York went into the Cathedral
St Winfords Church the Museum St Mareys Habbey went round York
Castle & the guild Hall & the City walls.

On Sunday September 27 1874 I went with Wm Haigh far Wortshill
to Halifax to hear a woman lecture on Spiritualism we went by white
lee top o hill, mosoldenedge, Rishworth Mill, slithro Bottom
Ripponden Tryangle, Sowerby Bridge, Skircoat and left Halifax at 9
oclock came back by West vale and Stainland and got home 5 minutes
to 12 at Night. Butifull Day.

1881 June 27 I went to see old Mrs Hirst of Digley Mill holmfirth and
also Grace Charlesworth who lived at Austoneley in Holmfirth. And she
was nearly 88 years of age when I saw her and Mrs Hirst of Digley
nearly 82 years of age. I set out from Wortshill at 25 minutes after ten in
the forenoon and got home at 10oclock at night. And I had a fine time
going and coming back. (James Hirst also visited Mrs Hirst in 1882,
1884, and 1886. By 1886 he was 73 years old and walked there and
back in one day. This was in June, presumably to maximise the
amount of daylight. The return trip would be between 16-18 miles.)

1887 June 8th I went to a Treat that was given to old Folks that was
above 64 years of age in the National school at Slaithwaite. And a
very good Treat it was a Knife and Fork tea and plenty of pipes and
Tobacco and Ale. There was plenty of speech making singing and
dansing And I liked very well.

The Cost of Living

Much has been said in the newspapers and at public meetings about the
greatly increased cost of living and every head of a family knows only too
well that is necessary expenses have recently increased at an alarming rate
the discussion respecting the present high prices of provisions have been
both interesting and usefull many economical housekeeping not the least
the curious contribution to the discussions is a letter which appeared in the
Leeds Mercury *last Tuesday giving a comparison between the cost of*

certain articles in 1871 &1816 the writer says:-.

*Having culled out at the beginning of the this year a few items of
a gentlemans expenses last year and in 1816 I take the liberty of
forwarding them and you the following five articles of one years
consumption by a family of four persons* [one man and three
women] *all grown up.*

	In 1871 £ s d			In 1816 £ s d		
Lump sugar	2	3	0	7	10	0
Raw sugar	2	10	10	8	10	0
	4	**13**	**10**	**16**	**0**	**0**
Tea	3	11	10	8	3	6
Soap	1	14	0	5	0	0
Flour	8	0	0	16	0	0
	17	19	9	45	3	6
Butchers Meat	11	17	9	0	0	0
Bacon	9	1	3	0	0	0
	38	18	11	38	18	11
				£6	**4**	**7**

*So that five articles of general consumption would cost less by £6 4s
7d than the four would have done in 1816 and this includes the whole
cost (not the difference only) of butchers meat & Bacon in 1816 Salt
was 5d a ld, Candles 1s 3d a ld* [no gas then], *Currants 1s 2d a ld
and Spices VC VC in proportion. Clothing too was especially cotton
goods were much dearer, A pair of mens stockings was 5s 6d, No dawn
hats fir to be seen under 22s or 23s each. All these may be fairly set
against dear meat and dear house rents.*

Notes and References

1. Groundling – a creeping or dwarf plant.
2. Gall stones.
3. Sulphur.
4. Rabies.
5. Recipe.
6. Standedge.
7. Rinderpest is an acute viral disease of cattle.
8. Delivered.
9. Chamber would have been the living-room kitchen.
10. Stewards of the Dartmouth estate.
11. Pole Moor Chapel.
12. Thatch.
13. James's younger brother, Edmund (b.1828) went to Cheethams but became a wastrel!
14. Fountain's Abbey.
15. Sowerby Bridge.

3. THE CENTRE OF LIGHT AND KNOWLEDGE: THORNTON'S TEMPERANCE HOTEL 1854-1909

by Alan J Brooke

IN OCTOBER 1909 THE *HUDDERSFIELD EXAMINER* announced the closure of *Thornton's Temperance Hotel*, which occupied the upper storey at 21 New Street, a site now occupied by Marks & Spencer's store (Figure 1). For over half a century it had provided a forum for local radicals, philosophers, scientists and poets to discuss religious and political subjects, or modern theories, frowned on elsewhere such as the Mechanics Institutes. Such was its influence on local intellectual and political activity that it earned itself the reputation, probably first coined with some sarcasm, as the

Figure 1. View of New Street showing location of *Thornton's* (upper storey) before Marks & Spencer's store was built on the site. *Kirklees Cultural Services, Huddersfield Local History Library.*

Figure 2. Joseph and Mary Thornton from an undated newspaper article on Thornton's by Stanley Chadwick. *Huddersfield Local History Library.*

'Centre of Light and Knowledge'. The names of over 130 local 'frequenters' are recorded, most of them self-employed tradesmen and small manufacturers, along with a smattering of farmers and schoolmasters. In 1875 one frequenter claimed that at least half of the councillors and aldermen of the town, and a fair proportion of members of the School Board and Board of Guardians, had been regular visitors to *Thornton's*. At the heart of this homespun intelligentsia was the 'hotel keeper' Joseph Thornton (Figure 2) and his circle of like-minded friends, veterans of the political campaigns of the 1830s and 1840s.[1]

Joseph was born in 1818 in Leeds and as a young man moved to Paddock where he worked as a cropper at Pedley's Mill. He became involved in the struggle against the New Poor Law and marched, and possibly fought, alongside Richard Oastler under the notorious black Paddock 'Bastille Flag'. As that movement merged into Chartism he became a supprter of Feargus O'Connor and attempted to put his Land Plan into effect by founding his own model farm. Although O'Connor aimed at settling workers on individual small-holdings, Joseph apparently saw no contradiction between this scheme and Socialism, as he was also a fervent admirer of Robert Owen. No one in Huddersfield was said to have a better grasp, not only of Owen's ideas, but also those of the French socialists, Saint-Simon, Fourier and Louis Blanc. He was also familiar with the writings of a now largely forgotten advocate of a co-operative economy, John Bellers (1654-1725). With the collapse of Socialism and Chartism in the late 1840s Joseph joined the Secularist movement which united the remnants of political reformers, socialists, co-operators, republicans and freethinkers into one body. [2]

Around the beginning of 1855 he acquired the *Temperance Hotel* on New Street which had been opened about five years before by Henry Wimpenny of Berry Brow, a tailor, reputed to have introduced the first sewing machine to Huddersfield. Whether or not Joseph acquired the hotel with a view to providing a suitable venue for Secularists, often banned from meeting halls, soon the Committee of the West Riding Secular Union (later Association), was meeting there. Joseph never appears as a leading organiser or platform speaker, but acted as treasurer for organisations, including the WRSU, a sign not only that he was trusted, but that he was at least comfortably off. He was able to afford a donation of ten shillings to the Secularists' national 'Special Institute Fund' in 1858. His wife Mary, born in Hartshead, and his only child, Sarah Ann, born in 1839, helped him with the running of the hotel. Possibly there were medical reasons why Mary could not bear other children. In the Burial Register for 11 October 1855 is the melancholy entry 'Joseph Thornton's child still born'. The father's occupation, 'Temperance Hotel keeper', leaving no doubt this is our Joseph. Sarah Ann lived on the premises with her husband, Samuel Bottom, a joiner and carpenter from Paddock, and two sons George (born 1860) and Joseph (1865). [3]

Joseph was not just a political animal but also a music lover. He taught and conducted a temperance fife and drum band. Edwin Swift of Linthwaite, a handloom weaver's son, was so inspired by Thornton's tuition that he went on to become a leading brass-band conductor and score arranger. Thornton was himself an accomplished flautists and French horn player in Old Moore's

Quadrille Band and his talent was deemed sufficient to judge brass band competitions at Belle Vue, Manchester. He also had a passion for literature, particularly Shakespeare and for football. [4]

The 'Frequenters'

One of Joseph's contemporaries, long associated with 'Thornton's', was William Armitage, born at Honley Woodbottom, near Crosland Factory in 1815. William practically imbibed his hatred of injustice with his mother's milk. The shock with which his mother greeted the news of the Peterloo massacre in 1819 left a profound impression on him. Begining work as a piecer in Wrigley's Mill at Netherton aged six he worked his way up to become an engineer, moving to Stoney Batter in South Crosland around 1837, where he lived until his death. His involvement in politics began with the agitation against child labour and for the *Ten Hour Bill*, which led him, as it did many others, towards Chartism. During the campaign for the Charter in 1839 he pledged to abstain from excisable items and never again smoked or drank. He was on the reception committee which met Feargus O'Connor on his release from York Castle in 1840 and developed such a fervent admiration for the Chartist leader that he earned himself the nickname 'Feargus O'Connor', which stuck with him for the rest of his life. Described simply as a 'Chartist operative' by the *Leeds Mercury* he raised questions about the separation of church and state at a meeting in the Philosophical Hall in 1847 (Figure 3). Armitage, who is referred to as an 'Engineer' in the 1851 census, was reputed to have been

Figure 3. This house which still bears the name Stoney Batter in the hamlet of South Crosland is where William Armitage, alias 'Feargus O'Connor' spent most of his adult life.

blacklisted for his opinions, perhaps explaining why in 1861 and 1871 he appears as a self-employed 'card dealer'. In 1859, almost a decade after the demise of the local Chartist movement, when he called for the whole Charter at a parliamentary reform meeting, he was still referred to by the *Huddersfield Chronicle* as 'Feargus O'Connor!' According to local historian D F E Sykes however, who probably knew him, William did not have the oratorical prowess of his hero,

> *...he was not a platform orator. He mainly confined himself to giving to and begging for the cause, to distributing literature, and to quiet, unobtrusive but caustic advocacy in private circles, or , in the declining years of his life, in the famous forum at 'Thornton's...*

He is mentioned speaking on at least two occasions during the agitation for the second Reform Bill in 1865-66, at meetings starring the former Chartist leader Ernest Jones.[5]

In 1847 William was reported in the Chartist paper *Northern Star* seconding a resolution against oppression in Ireland. Forty-two years later his passion for this cause was undiminished and he was among a group who held discussions with Irish MP William Redmond at Thornton's. Referring to the treatment of O'Brien MP and other Irish prisoners, Armitage (whom the *Examiner* still referred to as 'alias Feargus O'Connor'!), recollected how Chartist prisoners had once suffered similar degrading conditions.[6]

In 1885, for the first time in his life, he was able to cast a vote in a general election as a result of the *Reform Act* he had struggled so long to see. That year a presentation ceremony was held at *Thornton's* when he received a portrait of himself and two purses with cash totalling £26 18s. Fellow Thornton regular, Frank Curzon, dedicated a sonnet eulogising his principles,

> *...You recked not if you seem uncouth,*
> *But spoke out nobly for the good old cause-*
> *That rich and poor in right should brothers be:*
> *For all who breath in Britain -equal laws.*
> *This in some measure, you have lived to see;*
> *We think, speak, act in freedom. Let us pause.*
> *And thank you for your fearless fight for liberty.*

Among the causes he championed, apart from universal suffrage and Ireland, was the liberation of Poland and support for the North against the slave owners in the American Civil War. William Rowland Croft, another of Thornton's circle, dedicated his *History of the Factory Movement - or Oastler and His Times* to Armitage in 1888 as

'...one of the few surviving connecting links.' with that era of struggle.[7]

That link broke with Armitage's death in late November 1894. Two months later W R Croft, on his way home after a particularly exciting discussion evening at *Thornton's*, collapsed and died aged only fifty-eight. As well as being a local historian, Croft was active in local radical politics from the 1860s. A grocer at Rashcliffe, (working later as a commission agent while his wife ran the shop), he appealed in 1862 in a letter to the *Examiner*, which concluded with the rousing slogan *Roma o Morte*, for donations to support the wounded and gaoled Italian liberation fighter Garibaldi. Joseph Thornton acted as treasurer and he later received a signed photograph and letter of thanks when Garibaldi visited England in 1864. Croft was 'much indebted' in his views to John Stuart Mill, whose work *On Liberty* he frequently quoted in speeches or letters to the press. He was opposed to any interference in individual freedoms and opposed the Sabbatarian campaign to outlaw beer-selling on Sundays. His abhorrence of slavery led him to challenge the one-time Chartist and Secularist, Joseph Barker, speaking in 1863 on behalf of the pro-Confederate Southern Association. The meeting in the Philosophical Hall 'broke up in confusion' when Croft insisted that Barker give an explanation why his anti-Southern views, expressed in a letter from America in 1856, had changed. It is also probably Croft who signed himself 'W.R.C.' in a letter to the *Examiner* suggesting that Huddersfield operatives, made idle by the disruption of cotton supplies from America, should also benefit from the fund set up for distressed Lancashire cotton spinners.[8]

His constant support for the extension of the vote to working men also led him to become secretary of the Huddersfield branch of the National Reform League in 1865-66. He helped organise a demonstration in St Georges Square on 24 July 1866 addressed by Ernest Jones (Figure 4). The Thorntonites, W Armitage, F Curzon, W White and Charles Denham, (possibly including a John Thornton, who may be Joseph's brother of that name), as well as Croft himself, spoke in favour of an extension of the *Reform Bill* to encompass 'Residential Manhood Suffrage'.[9]

Croft's international interests extended from the Balkans to France. He was involved in the widespread local protest meetings against Turkish atrocities in Bulgaria in 1876 and led conducted tours of the sites of battlefields of the Franco-Prussian war, helped by his ability to speak French. Ireland was another perennial issue and in 1889, along with Armitage and other regulars, he met William Redmond MP at *Thornton's*. Moving the resolution of support, he commented

For thirty or thirty five years that room had echoed to the voices of men who had played a part, though it might be an obscure part, in the struggle for freedom... .

Among those voices were three in particular who, in different ways, were to have an influence on the life of Huddersfield.[10]

Watts Balmforth, born in Slaithwaite in 1826, worked first at Fishers silk factory then at Starkey's, Longroyd Bridge. He moved from Manchester Road to Rashcliffe becoming a machine knife grinder at the Engine Bridge Machine Works at Folly Hall. In the 1871 census he is described as a 'mechanic'. A keen vegetarian as well as temperance adherent, he was, like Joseph Thornton, an admirer of Robert Owen, so much so that he called his eldest son

Figure 4. Thorntonites like W R Croft planned and spoke at this demonstration advertised in the *Huddersfield Examiner* of 21 July 1866. Ernest Jones and Edmund Beales were among the national celebrities said to have stayed at the hotel.

OPEN AIR REFORM DEMONSTRATION.

SATURDAY, July 21st, 1866.

UNDER THE AUSPICES OF THE REFORM LEAGUE.

A MASS MEETING will be held in St. George's Square, THIS DAY (SATURDAY), to take into consideration the present state of reform movement, and the Advent of a Tory Adminstration to power.

EDMOND BEALES, Esq.,
Of London, president of the Reform League.

ERNEST JONES, Esq.,
Barrister at Law.

ALDERMAN CARTER,
Leeds.

E. O. GREENING, Esq.,
Manchester.

and other gentlemen are expected to be present, and address the meeting

Chair to be taken at five o'clock.

REFORMERS ATTEND IN THOUSANDS.

Owen. Along with Joseph he was on the committee of the West Riding Secular Association in the 1850s and took part in Reform League activities in the 1860s. Lockwood Mechanics' Institute, the Lowerhead Row Co-operative Society and the Friendly and Trades Societies Club all benefited from his involvement. In a letter to the *Examiner* in 1889 he strongly contested Tory claims that coercive powers dealing with unrest in Ireland were any less severe than those under Gladstone. His sons Owen and Ramsden, though not directly mentioned in relation to Thornton's, were also prominent in local Secularist, Republican and Radical organisations and must have attended discussions there. Owen continued in the tradition of radical liberalism, eventually being elevated to Mayor, while Ramsden, who became a Unitarian minister, was involved in the revival of the Labour and Socialist movement until his emigration to South Africa in 1894.[11]

Frank Curzon, originally from Devon, is best known for his association with Huddersfield Mechanics' Institute, which he served as secretary between 1854 and 1862. He was also organising secretary of the Yorkshire Union of Mechanics' Institutes and in 1883 co-authored *Huddersfield: A Short Description of the Town...* for delegates to a conference here. One former student and *Thornton's* frequenter, John Blackburne, concluded that

> *Mr Curzon's labours in the cause of education had been of incalculable benefit to the neigbourhood.*

Curzon had met Robert Owen, whom he admired as a great social pioneer, and along with other Thorntonites was involved with Huddersfield Reform League, chairing, in 1865, a meeting at the Gymnasium addressed by Ernest Jones. He was so closely associated with *Thornton's* that it was joked that as a correspondent for the *Leeds Mercury* his reports on the state of the cloth trade were based on what manufacturers ordered for dinner there – meat and potatoes meant trade was flourishing, coffee and a bun that it was depressed. He was remembered as a 'very amusing lecturer... ever true to art, education and good fellowship.' A specimen of his wit is preserved in a report of a dinner speech at *Thornton's* in October 1898, when, aged eighty, he was a guest along with other 'veteran attenders',

> *...he owed more to that room than it could possibly owe to him. He had had the misfortune to be a stump orator for nearly 60 years and before he went to deliver an address anywhere he came to that room, for he got there ideas so original and mysterious that when he gave his lectures people were 'flabbergasted'.* (Laughter)

The story of BENJAMIN SHAW & SONS LTD and their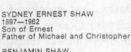

Great-grandfather
BENJAMIN SHAW
1835—1901
The founder of the
business in 1871.

From left to right
BEAUMONT STEPHENSON
1877—1948
Ben's first office boy in 1891
Director 1924, Father of Clifford

ERNEST SHAW
1860—1924
Ben's elder son

FRANK SHAW
1872—1946
Ben's younger son

SYDNEY ERNEST SHAW
1897—1962
Son of Ernest
Father of Michael and Christopher

BENJAMIN SHAW
1902—1969
Son of Frank
Father of Terry and Martin

To these, our predecessors, who in their day were as enterprising
and progressive as we strive to be; whose principles of making
high quality products marketed competitively were the foundations
on which the Company has built and expanded, we, the fourth generation, Directors, pay tribute

Figure 5. Benjamin Shaw and his dynasty, suppliers of non-alcoholic beverages. Shaw himself was a great frequenter of *Thornton's*.

He also entertained people with his drawings and verse - a sample of the latter is recorded in the sonnet to W Armitage partly reproduced above.[12]

Someone whose career took a different course due to association with *Thornton's* was Benjamin Shaw. The story of how he trundled his hand-cart with non-alcoholic botanic porter and ginger beer to *Thornton's*, thus founding his mineral water empire has been oft told (Figure 5). Less recognised are his political interests. Born in 1836 at Fenay Bridge he worked as a woollen spinner until he began his new business in 1871. He was a member of both the Reform League, speaking at the St George's Square meeting in 1866, and the Republican Club, chairing a meeting in 1875 at the Cambridge Temperance Hall on the 'Land Question'. Like many self educated men he was eager to promote intellectual and moral improvement, advocating in a letter to the *Chronicle* the founding of a Working Man's Club in Huddersfield, congenial to informed discussion, with a reading room, library, smoking room and games room, but prohibiting betting and, of course, 'no intoxicating liquors are allowed on the premises'. Described in his obituary in 1901 as 'a great frequenter of *Thornton's*', it was said to be there that he first met town councillors and became interested in municipal affairs. Unlike some other frequenters, however, his Radical and Republican views mellowed, becoming an opponent of Home Rule for Ireland and joining the Unionist Liberals in 1885. He was elected to the council, but he is better known as a founder of the Yorkshire Mineral Water Manufacturers' Association which pioneered in Huddersfield a 'bottle exchange' to collect bottles for re-use.[13]

Other 'frequenters' who have left less of a record include Samuel Mitchell one of Joseph Thornton's comrades from his Owenite and Chartist days. Mitchell, born in 1815 started work as a bobbin winder and drawboy for a handloom weaver, was employed at Starkey's factory and in 1854 opened a grocery business in Portland Street. A lifelong supporter of freethought in 1886 he was treasurer of Huddersfield Secularist Society. He apparently visited the US in 1887 and at the meeting with W Redmond MP at *Thornton's* in 1889 he referred to the irony that while the Irish were prominent in American politics they had little say in the running of their own country. Along with contemporary William Sykes he was a guest at the veterans dinner in 1898. Described after his death as 'strong in Radical faith', it was said he would insist on paying for a glass of water as a contribution to the hotel. Charles Denham, a leather currier, one of the speakers at the 1866 Reform demonstration, bought more than water – he claimed in 1876 to have taken dinner and tea at *Thornton's* almost every day since it opened![14]

Visiting Celebrities
As well as the frequenters, the names of over thirty occasional stayers at the hotel of national renown are recorded. They include Socialists, Chartists, Co-operators, Secularists, Republicans, Radicals, Liberals and single issue missionaries. The most famous, and a close personal friend of Joseph Thornton, was Charles Bradlaugh, known as 'Iconoclast', radical, republican and leader of the secularist movement for around thirty years. A former frequenter who worked at the *Examiner* office later recollected visiting *Thornton's* one evening for supper and being shown into the parlour by Sarah to find a full bath-tub and all the chairs ranged in front of a roaring fire, warming a complete outfit of clothes, which she explained belong to Bradlaugh. It was the orator's habit to have a bath and a complete change of clothes when he finished a meeting. This apparently happened in the 1880s but Bradlaugh visited the town at least fifteen times, and

possibly more, between 1860 and 1890, usually staying at *Thornton's*. Credit for first inviting him was claimed by David Woofenden (1813-1892) a bill poster and newsagent of Lockwood who sold secularist and radical literature in the Shambles open market. In recognition of his work he was presented with a portrait of himself in a ceremony at the Secular Institute on East Parade in 1884.[15]

Bradlaugh, along with a constellation of Secularists celebrities, addressed a massive meeting at Castle Hill in July 1860 and again in 1874. Several times he spoke at the Philosophical Hall, or the Theatre Royal as it became in 1866. November that year saw one of the more lively events there. Booked one Sunday to deliver three lectures – 'Temperance', 'Reform' and 'The Twelve Apostles' – Bradlaugh and his supporters arrived in the morning to find themselves locked out in the rain by the owner, opposed to infidel preaching. In the afternoon he returned with a crowbar and forced open the Bull and Mouth Street entrance, only to be arrested before he could commence his speech. As an angry crowd gathered outside the police offices Sam Mitchell and William Armitage sped off in a cab to try and arrange magistrate's bail, while Bradlaugh appealed to his supporters to disperse and vacate the occupied theatre. Charged with twenty-four shillings (£1.20p) damage to the door and a breach of the peace he conducted his own courtroom defence and was acquitted 'amid great confusion and clash of tongues'.[16]

Topics he lectured on included Ireland (1868 and 1887), and (chaired by Ben Shaw in 1877) the population question, which covered controversial views on birth control. On 11 October 1884, now a MP, he was in Huddersfield addressing a massive Reform Bill demonstration, (which flew banners invoking the heady days of agitation for the first *Reform Bill* in 1832), and packed out meetings in the Armoury and Town Hall. He was to visit the town, and no doubt *Thornton's*, at least four more times before his death in early 1891.[17]

On at least one occasion, 1878 when he spoke on 'the Eastern Question', Bradlaugh visited Huddersfield with his close colleague, Annie Besant, who is also mentioned as staying at *Thornton's*. Other Secularists or former Owenites who visited the hotel include G J Holyoake and his brother Austin, John Watts, Isaac Ironside, Lloyd Jones, Harriet Law, William Maccall and the eccentric Joseph Barker, mentioned above, whose career ranged from Methodism (New Connexion), through Chartism to Secularism and back to Methodism (Primitive). Another stayer was Robert Cooper a former Socialist who briefly lived in Huddersfield in the late 1840s.[18]

The list of Radicals and parliamentary reformers said to have stayed runs like a role-call of the surviving leaders of the Chartist movement. As well as Ernest Jones, there was Henry Vincent, Thomas Cooper, George J Harney, Bronterre O'Brien, Samuel Kydd and R C Gammage. Irish Home Rule MPs include William Redmond, John O Connor and J C Biggar, the latter demanding the release of all Fenian prisoners at a meeting in 1877. Other personalities include David Urquhart, obsessed by a conspiracy theory of Russia's plan for world domination; C Dobson Collett, secretary of the society against the tax on newspapers (a cause dear to many Thorntonites); Edmund Beales and George Howell, president and secretary of the National Reform League; and Joseph Arch the agricultural labourers union leader.[19]

The Light Goes Out

Not everyone who frequented the hotel was sympathetic to the views of Thornton and his group. Some came knowing they could have a good argument, others came to discuss artistic, literary or scientific topics, or just to play chess or draughts in a congenial atmosphere. One 'Mr Calvert, the painter, was a very strong Tory,' it was recollected,

> When he had 'fratched' his best, and could stand the Radicals no longer, he used to rush out of the room in a great temper, using very strong language... .

Joseph Thornton was renowned for dealing with such situations. At a surprise testimonial presentation on eve 1875 (where Joseph and Mary were presented with portraits and a marble clock with a dedicatory inscription), a close friend, John Blamires, paid tribute to

> the uniform attention he [Thornton] had given to all classes of persons who attended the house, where both employer and employed, all classes of politicians, all sects of theologians often met, and many times he had heard political conversations commenced which had warmed up into hot discussions and sometimes to personal remarks. Then their host dropped in a jocular remark, which acted like oil on troubled waters.[20]

He also referred to Joseph's 'irony, sarcasm and wit' in conversation. Thornton also had a mischievous sense of humour and entertained patrons with his amusing recitals, however no one was in doubt about his erudition and the sincerity of his deeply held beliefs. His death left a great void and it was perhaps partly as a result of the loss of his conciliatory influence that one of the resident bards, objecting to the level of acrimonious debate, left an anonymous satirical 'Sonnet to Thornton's' on the mantle-piece of the smoking room on the anniversary of Shakespeare's birthday in 1890. It concluded:

> '... *Yet still retain thine intellectual might -*
> *Learn to restrain thy wild tempestuous brood,*
> *And let Love's lamp aye keep thy steps aright!*
> *For satire fierce and declamation rude,*
> *Scarcely are Knowledge, and still less are Light!*'[21]

Following the death of Mary in March 1886 Joseph's health declined rapidly and he died on 3 October 1887 from a combination of illnesses. He was buried alongside Mary in Huddersfield Cemetery two days later. The procession of Thorntonites including Armitage, William White and Ben Shaw left the *Temperance Hotel*. W R Croft was himself recovering from a serious illness and confined to a carriage. The service was conducted by the Rev. Rawlings of the Unitarian Chapel, Fitzwilliam Street, who read lines from one of Joseph's favourite poets, William Cullen Bryant. On the coffin was a large wreath, *A Tribute of Respect from Frequenters of Thornton's*. His obituary commented that his 'comrades in arms' and others would feel, 'that the light has gone out at *Thornton's*'.[22]

Sarah Bottom ran the hotel for a while until a number of frequenters formed the Thornton's Temperance Hotel Company Ltd and employed George Judson as manager. There was still a vibrant intellectual atmosphere and in 1894 the Thornton's Temperance Hotel Literary and Scientific Society was formed with Joseph Rayner and Henry Weintz as president and secretary. But in 1896 the *Yorkshire Factory Times* 'snapshot' column lamented the passing of Thornton, Armitage, Croft and others, 'some of the brilliance of the place is departed... . True and good company goes yet but not the same company as ten years ago.'[23]

Part of the decline is attributable to the growing popularity of some of the very ideas espoused at *Thornton's*. However, a new generation such as those who wrote for and read the *Factory Times*, like the weavers' union leaders Ben Turner and Allen Gee, saw the realisation of their aspirations in Socialism. Turner recollected fondly,

> *Thornton's was a regular debating place and when I used to go there one could learn about politics, science, religion and social topics, including town affairs.*

Symptomatic of the sea change which was taking place at a national level, Annie Besant broke with Bradlaugh and Secularism. She visited the town as a missionary of the Fabian Society in February

1887, to speak on 'The Message of Socialism' at the Friendly and Trades Club. In October of that year William Morris of the Socialist League spoke at the Victoria Hall. Around this time, or possibly even earlier, a local Fabian Society was established becoming,

> *undoubtedly the first organised effort in the direction of Socialism. Its members were few in number and so meagre were its resources that it was perforce compelled to hold its meetings in that well known temperance hotel called Thornton's ...the members being cordially welcome to discuss the ideals of Fabianism without paying rent beyond the purchase of a cup of tea or coffee 'for the good of the house'.*

D F E Sykes also records that local Fabians first met in *Thornton's* after a visit by William de Mattos in 1890, but it is clear that the Socialist revival was already well under way. Sadly, there is no record of what the old Owenite Socialists thought of the new ideas, or how their views influenced young men like Turner and Ramsden Balmforth. One result of the resurgence of Socialism was the creation of new clubs and a new political culture which passed *Thornton's* by.[24]

The links with the past were severed one by one. Sam Mitchell died in 1900 and Ben Shaw (Figure 6) the following year. In 1902, at a presentation to the retiring managers Mr and Mrs Abraham Crossley, John Blackburne declared himself now the oldest frequenter of the hotel. In 1904 Watts Balmforth died and the next year John Culley. The latter, born in Almondbury in 1823, had been a fancy cloth designer who had worked in America before returning to Huddersfield in 1860 to open *Culley's Temperance Hotel*. He then became a cloth dealer on Cross Church Street. A radical 'of the old school', according to his obituary, he spent 'a good deal of his unoccupied time discussing politics and other subjects in the front room of *Thornton's*...'. But by now the political influence of *Thornton's* had decreased and it was mainly a debating society. Its role as a temperance house was also emphasised more, since from about 1897 it was the headquarters of James Firth's Huddersfield and District Temperance League.[25]

On 5 October 1909 another William Armitage who 'was for a great number of years a well-known and welcome visitor at *Thornton's*' died aged sixty. He was a pit manager at Fieldhouse Colliery, a Liberal, a Wesleyan and honorary secretary of the Thornton's Temperance Hotel Company whose chairman, Alderman Andrew Chatterton, attended the funeral. Less than three weeks later the obituary appeared for *Thornton's* itself, which finally closed its doors on 23 October. Some of the 'Ex-Thorntonites' continued to meet in

Robinson's Café, where, in March 1910, a lecture was delivered by an anti-Socialist campaigner, Bradford stonemason Robert Dawson, followed by a discussion with local Socialists.[26]

The physical atmosphere of *Thornton's,*

> *converse warm and wild, wise and witty, whimsical and windy, of deeply studied and keenly fought games of draughts and chess, of cups of coffee, hot , strong and aromatic, consumed in clouds of smoke of the fragrant weed, and of humorous anecdotes.*

may have been possible to recreate, but not the intellectual excitement of its heyday. A few lines of strained and archaic verse, dedicated to the veterans at their reception in 1898, described their resilience, and that of other Thorntonites, in keeping alive the struggle for social and political reform throughout the nineteenth century:

Figure 6. Headstone of Benjamin Shaw, buried at South Crosland church in the same grave as his first wife, Elizabeth, and their five children.

...Centred within
Their memories Huddersfield's history
Still shines with coruscating brilliance,
And to the younger generation gives,
An impetus to loyalty and truth
Which must rejuvenate remembrance.
On, on into hopeful futurity,
Singly, in pairs, or in full company,
Move after move they made on life's great board,
Attacking and attacked; defeated now,
*– **And then victorious...*** [27]

Notes and References

1. I would like to thank the staff of Huddersfield Local History Library (HLHL) and West Yorkshire Archive Service (Kirklees), in particular, Lesley Kipling, for support during my rresearch. The local political background to this article can be found in the closing chapters of Brooke, A J 'The Hall of Science' (Huddersfield 1993) and the national context in E Royle

Victorian Infidels (Manchester 1974). Account of closure of Thorntons: *Huddersfield Examiner* (Weekly) (HEW) 30 Oct 1909; 6 Nov 1909, reprinted in Parkin's *Almanac* 1925.

2.Thornton's obituaries are in HEW and *HuddersfieldWeekly News,* 8 October 1887; For the Chartist background see Brooke A J 'The Whole Hog' Chapter 3, *Aspects of Huddersfield,* I Schofield, editor (Barnsley 1999).

3. *The Reasoner,* 4 Nov 1855; 26 May, 5 Sep 1858; Royle *op cit.* p. 227. Census 1861, three female servants and one boarder are also recorded at the premises; Huddersfield Cemetery, Register of Burials 1855.

4. Swift's obituary, HEW 13 Mar 1904.

5. Obituary HEW 2 Dec 1893; Stoney Batter Chartist, *Huddersfield Echo,* 20 Aug 1887; *Leeds Mercury,* 6 Nov 1847; census of 1851; 1861; 1871. *Huddersfield Chronicle,* (HC) 19 Mar 1859; D F E Sykes, *History of Huddersfield andVicinity,* p302; HC 9 Sep 1865; HC 28 Jul 1866.

6. *Northern Star,* 18 Dec 1847; HEW 9 Feb 1898.

7. *Huddersfield Echo,* 20 Aug 1887.

8. Obituary HEW 3 Feb 1894; census of 1881; HEW 27 Sep 1862 (Garibaldi); HEW 13 Dec 1862; HEW 30 Jan 1864 (Sunday beer selling); HEW 26 Sep 1863 (Barker); HEW 14 Nov 1863, (Cotton operatives).

9. HC 24 Sep 1866; HC 28 Jul 1866.

10. Obituary; HEW 16 Sep 1876 (Turkish atrocities); HEW 9 Feb 1889 (Redmond MP).

11. Obituary HEW 30 Jan 1904; HEW 9 Mar 1889; HEW 22 Oct 1906 (Owen); *Yorkshire Factory Times* (YFT) 26 Jun 1896 (Ramsden). Owen also became a Unitarian. See, for example, J O'Connell, 'From Mechanics Institute to Polytechnic' in *Huddersfield – a Most HandsomeTown,* H Haigh ed (Huddersfield 1992); HEW 9 Sep 1865; HEW 22 Oct 1898 (Veterans).

13. Obituary, HEW, HC 16 Mar 1901: HEW 6 Mar 1875; HEW 15 Sep 1877.

14. Obituary HEW 25 Aug 1900; the reference to his departure to the US is in Thornton's obituary; HEW 1 Jan 1876 Denham speaks at Thornton Testimonial presentation.

15. Story of Bradlaugh s clothes is in HEW 6 Nov 1909; HEW 4 Oct 1884, Woofenden, for his obituaries – HEW and *HWN* 8 Oct 1892.

16. HEW 28 Feb 1860; Royle op.cit p.189; HEW 11 Jul 1874; H Bradlaugh-Bonner, Charles Bradlaugh *A Record of his Life andWork by his Daughter,* pp.240-243 (London 1908); HEW 1 Dec 1866.

17. H. Bradlaugh-Bonner *op cit.* p.260-261 this lecture on 25 August 1867 was the first memory his daughter, Hypatia, then aged ten, had of her father lecturing, the eager sympathetic faces, of the Huddersfield audience, and an old man in the front row with an ear trumpet; *Huddersfield Echo* 18 Jun 1887; HEW 15 Sep 1877; HEW 14 Oct 1884; Bradlaugh's obituary HEW 31 Jan 1891 says his last visit to Huddersfield was on 21 Sep 1890.

18. HEW 16 Mar 1878; for potted biographies of some of these see Royle *op cit* Appendix V. For Cooper, Brooke, *Hall of Science;* Holyoake visited in 1857 and left his own account, including a trip to the town's pleasant cemetery, *Reasoner* 11 Jan, 15 Feb 1857; for Barker s visits HE 28 Feb 1860; HE 28 Dec 1861.

19. John O'Connor's visit to town in HEW 8 Feb 1890; Biggar, HEW 24 Mar 1877; Arch, HEW 30 Nov 1872, HEW 30 Jan 1875.

20. HEW 30 Oct 1909; HEW 1 Jan 1876.

21. HEW 26 Apr 1890, the poet signed himself 'Censor'. As well as Curzon, a number of Thorntonites had poetic aspirations. One, J Donkersley, wrote a satire *Thornton's Gallery of Portraits* about other frequenters. W E Thomas wrote under the name 'Viator' for the *Examiner.* Both were schoolmasters.

22. Burial register, 25 March 1886, MaryThornton aged 69; Obituaries HEW and HWN 8 Oct 1887; an obituary also occurred in the National Secular Society's National Reformer according to HEW 22 Oct, but I have been unable to obtain this.

23. HEW 30 Oct 1909; census of 1891 shows George N Judson, aged 36, manager, born Kirkby Moorside, his wife Mary, 48, from Tordmorden and three sons of school age, born in Brighouse, plus two servants, two boarders and two visitors;YFT 26 Jun 1896.

24. B Turner, *About Myself,* p82; For A Besant *Huddersfield Echo,* 18 Jun, 8 Oct 1887; Morris HEW 13 Nov 1887; Handbook to ILP Conference, quoted in *Huddersfield Citizen* 20 Apr 1928, D F E Sykes, *History of Huddersfield and theValleys of the Colne, Home and Dearne,* pp.448-9. 25. HEW 6 May 1905.

26. HEW 9 Oct 1909; HEW 19 Mar 1910.

27. HEW 30 Oct 1909.

Acknowledgements

I am grateful to Kirklees Library Services for the picture of New Street, and to I H F Gibbs, Managing Director of Ben Shaws, for permission to use the advertising page.

4. WOOL, WAR AND THE INDIES: THE FISHER LETTERS

by Ian Sargen

AS THE LIGHT BEGAN TO FAIL at the end of an autumn afternoon in 1958, a group of Mothers' Union members, including my mother, was clearing up after a Jumble Sale at St Chad's Church, Ladybarn, Manchester. She came across a dirty brown-paper package, and was about to put it in the dustbin, when she noticed several old letters inside the wrapping.

From this package emerged a remarkably clear view of the life, feelings, and adventures of the Fisher family, who lived in Almondbury between the 1790s and the 1830s. Many of the letters were written home by the children of the family to their father, but some contain sombre news of the deaths of two sons. Taken overall, they show a local family playing a significant part in the technological advance of the West Riding, in its commercial development, in the mighty battles of the Peninsular War and Waterloo, and in Britain's empire-building in the West Indies. Apart from the twenty-four letters, all that remains of the family is twenty-six lines of lettering on a gravestone in All Hallows' churchyard, Almondbury (Figure 1), fleeting references in church records in Yorkshire and the Isle of Man, and brief mentions in army records in the Public Record Office at Kew.

Joseph Fisher and his family lived at Birks, a substantial farmhouse lying in fields sloping down from the village of Almondbury towards the Rushfield Dike, over two miles from

Figure 1. All Hallows' Church, Almondbury, where the Fisher family are buried. *Kirklees Cultural Services*

Figure 2. Birks, Almondbury, in 1905. *Kirklees Cultural Services*

Huddersfield (Figure 2). The farmhouse, stone-built and slate-roofed, was already two hundred years old. It was home to at least three families in the 1790s, and, like so many local houses, consisted of both farm buildings and weaving workshops. Fisher's landlord was the Earl of Dartmouth, Lord Chamberlain to King George III.

Joseph Fisher lived in the house from the 1790s until his death in 1837 at the age of seventy-nine. He had worked in London in his youth, but was established by 1798 as a manufacturer of 'kerseymears', using finer quality wool than the traditional local product, and the letters include an 1805 invoice for 662lbs of Spanish wool imported through Bristol. He had married his first wife, Nancy, by 1782, and they had six children. The only daughter, Susannah, died in 1811 at the age of twenty; a son, Mark, died before he was two in 1796; and for a time, it seemed that the second son, William, would also die early. He was having difficulty walking at the age of thirteen, and one of the letters in the collection is from Nancy, who had gone with William and Susannah to Matlock Bath to 'drink the waters', both for William's benefit, and for her own. She had been ill for at least eighteen months, and died back home only three months later in November, 1799, aged thirty-eight. Replying to his wife's letter from Matlock, Joseph says that he has met the local doctor, who has advised a long stay in Derbyshire: but the doctor, Robert Rockley Batty, himself died before Nancy did, drowned whilst attempting to swim across the Calder.

Joseph married his second wife, Mary, about ten years later, and had five further children. Four sons died in infancy, and the only survivor was a daughter, also called Mary, who died in 1832, when she was twenty-three.

The Fishers lived in disturbed and tumultuous times. The French Revolution and the Napoleonic Wars had a profound effect on life at every level in Great Britain, and her army and navy were active in many parts of the world. At home, there was real economic gloom, and Joseph wrote to his cousin in 1798: 'I am very sencible that our present State as a Nation is very Dark and Gloomy'. Disturbances were common in the West Riding throughout the period, with bread riots in 1799, as well as the Luddite riots thirteen years later, when local feelings ran very high, culminating in the murder of the local mill-owner, William Horsfall. Local workers suffered severe food shortages until the 1840s, and disease and poverty took its toll.

At the same time, the Almondbury and Huddersfield area showed a remarkable capacity for inventiveness. Its rapidly growing population found work in the new mills and 'manufacturies', which were developing new techniques and technologies. Almondbury, though by now eclipsed in population by Huddersfield, was nevertheless the centre of many new developments, including the use of silk, and, in the 1820s, the 'fancy trade'.

Joseph Fisher had a part in the new technology. His workshops at Birks evidently proved too small, and in 1801, together with nineteen other shareholders, he financed and built Birks Mill (Figures 3 & 4) at the bottom of the field below Birks. The Dartmouth Estate Book

Figure 3. Almondbury from the south-east, with Birks Mill on the left, 1891. *Kirklees Cultural Services*

Figure 4. Birks Mill from the north-east, 1905. *Kirklees Cultural Services*

of 1805 describes it as 'a large, Fulling, Scribbling, and Carding Mill'. The flow of water in Rushfield Dike proved quite insufficient for the mill, and Joseph and his partners were the first in the district to install a steam engine, apparently fed with coal from a small mine nearby at Dogley.

Along with his wool-making activities, Joseph also farmed his land, talking in August, 1799, of having '14 or 15 hands in the hay'. He was evidently a busy and successful man, though he put it more modestly: 'I spends my time in looking after my diferant buisnes'.

His eldest son, Thomas, obviously thought his father had no shortage of money ('he would find no loss of it'), and Joseph's later role as a Trustee of the new National School in Almondbury in 1818, and as a Churchwarden of All Hallows, Almondbury, from 1823 to 1826, suggests he prospered. The letters show him to be a stern paterfamilias. His style was extraordinarily old-fashioned, even for 1799, not only using the archaic 'thee' and 'thou', but also exhibiting a robust religious tone: 'See thou dost not offend Him,' he writes to his ailing thirteen year-old son, William, 'by an ungrateful Spirit and disposition but remember that he that being often reproved hardeneth his neck shall suddenly be destroyed and that without remedy.'

His dealings with Thomas show him as determined and decidedly obstinate. Thomas was born in 1782, and, according to his army records, became a 'clothdresser', doubtless in the family business at Birks. It is clear from the letters that Thomas sowed his wild oats, and in 1804, when he was twenty-two, he disgraced himself in the village. Whether the problem was girls, drinking, or bad company, or all three, is not clear from the letters, but it caused him to be packed off to join the 51st Regiment of Foot in Northallerton. He begs his father to take no notice of local gossip about him and 'M Scott', and says he is willing to 'drop all acquentance at that house any time – for I have had a great deal of blame for going to that house'. As time went on, Thomas developed a capacity for combining repeated apologies for his 'bad conduct' with recriminations against his father for not forgiving him. Thomas's reasons for enlisting were not unusual, and the Peninsular army largely consisted of young men escaping the results of their own excesses. In his melodramatic way, Thomas tells his father that he has told his younger brothers that 'they had better dash thier brains out than do as I have done'.

Thomas was immediately miserable in the army. Life there was harsh, and Thomas missed home. Enlisting brought a bounty, but that was soon eaten up in paying off the recruiting sergeant, buying kit, and paying for food. Army records show that he was receiving the regulation one shilling per day, with eighty-one pence per quarter in lieu of beer. He wrote home almost immediately pleading for money, so that he could buy decent kit (the regimental issue was 'worth nothing at all and ... made in the slightest manner'). A year later, he was still pleading: 'If you will send me 1£ it will reliev very much'. Thomas could not resist voicing his resentment against his father, however, and he complains that 'if you had the thought for me that a father ought to have you would wish me to do a little better.' He admits to being a 'prodigal', but cannot resist complaining that 'there are men that would not be so hard as you'. He suggests that he might go to the Indies, and 'try what I can do amongst the blacks'. This would have meant either desertion, which was not uncommon, or paying to be discharged. Even in 1810, after the Corunna Campaign, Thomas is still begging his father to pay for a discharge. Thomas was unlucky, however: when his father finally agreed to apply on his behalf through the Earl of Dartmouth, the Earl died before the letter could be written. In late 1810, he got as far as being questioned by his Commanding Officer, Colonel Mainwaring, who had been told that Thomas's father 'was a young man in the prime of his life [who] had lately married a second wife'. Thomas indignantly protested that his father 'was now upwards of 50 Years of age and that your age not only rendered you incapable of looking after your Biusness but also of keeping your Books of accounts'!

Thomas did not get his discharge, for two other good reasons: he was now in the Regimental Band, and the 51st was about to return to Spain and Portugal, both of which factors made him indispensable.

When Thomas enlisted, the main body of the 51st Regiment was in Ceylon, returning home only in 1807, seriously depleted by tropical disease. In 1808, it consisted of 'volunteers from the Militia [and] raw recruits with a few old soldiers'. Nevertheless, the 51st was sent in that year to Spain with its former colonel, Sir John Moore. Once there, the British Army was heavily outnumbered by Napoleon's troops, and Moore took his troops back through the rigours of a harsh winter in Northern Spain to the coast at Corunna, and to the safety of the Royal Navy's fleet of warships and transports. Moore himself was killed at Corunna, and the campaign was, in Thomas's words, 'one of the hardest campaigns that any British soldier before experienc'd where I may safely say that I was one out of ten escaped the Hand of Death.' The 'unsufferable Hardships and fatigue where Men who I once thought were able to undergo Double the fatigue of me' did not exaggerate the suffering of the army and its camp-followers in the heavy rain and snows of January, 1809.

Thomas's military career had not been helped by the fact that he was flogged in 1807, apparently for falling asleep on guard duty. Even then, Thomas explains to his brother that 'I should not have had a lash if our officers could have indered [hindered] it, but it was not in their hands for I was tried by a Garrison cort Marshall.'

After Corunna, the 51st was made into a 'Light Infantry' Regiment, and fought in the disastrous Walcheren Campaign of 1809 in the Netherlands, where malaria reduced the fighting strength of the Regiment to almost half. Thomas again seems to have survived. He writes on one occasion from Croydon, where the Regiment had been sent to put down imminent civil disorder in London, and he mentions the persistent rumours that the 51st was destined for Spain and Portugal ('Portingale') again.

By this time, he is calmer in his tone, although he says that he 'cannot expect to escape much longer – I find myself much infirm'd by the hardships I have already suffered.' In the next eight years, he accompanied the 51st through the long Peninsular Campaign, when regimental numbers sank to less than 300. By chance, even though Thomas does not write home to describe his adventures, several of the best firsthand accounts of the Peninsular War were written by men of the 51st Regiment, all of whom must have known Thomas. Among the most vivid are those of Colonel Samuel Rice, who countersigned some of Thomas's letters, and Private Wheeler; but Colonel Mainwaring's nephew, Frederick, who joined the regiment at the age of thirteen, chronicled his adventures in Spain and Portugal, and Major David Roberts, who, Thomas says, was living in Wakefield with his family in 1807, wrote the *The Adventures of Johnny Newcome*, a thinly-disguised account of his adventures with the 51st. Rice often voices the frustration of the ordinary soldier, who was ordered to march, starve, and fight, but who did not know the reason why: 'The Great Duke knows, but we poor devils know nothing.'

For the soldiers, there was continual hardship, in summer heat as well as in winter cold. Often there was no bread, and only 'bad biscuit', and they slept in the open until late in the campaign. The opportunities for pleasure were few, and overindulged in when they arrived. Drunkenness was an ever-present problem amongst the men, particularly in the vineyards of Northern Spain. Doubtless Thomas was one of the '12000 men... in a state of helpless inebriety' at Duenas.

In spite of Wellington's low opinion of his army ('the scum of the earth'), the 51st's reputation grew as the Peninsular War advanced. Matters were not initially helped by an incident at the Battle of Fuentes d'Onoro (Figure 5), when Colonel Mainwaring, Thomas's commanding officer, was court-martialled and sent home after

Figure 5. The Battle of Fuentes d'Onoro, 1811, in which Thomas Fisher fought. *Courtesy of the Director, National Army Museum*

Figure 6. The British Army bivouacking, Vilha Velha, Portugal, 1811. *Courtesy of the Director, National Army Museum*

burning the regiment's colours, believing them to be in danger from the French. Nevertheless, by the end of the campaign, Wellington was regularly complimenting the 51st on its contribution in the fierce sieges of Badajoz, the capture of Madrid, and the Battles of Burgos, Valladolid, Vittoria, Lesaca, and the Nivelle (Figure 6). The 51st fought its way north into France in 1814, went home, but was then sent to Belgium in 1815 when Napoleon escaped from Elba. At Waterloo, Thomas and the 51st withstood a fierce onslaught from the French at Hougoumont before the battle was won.

Thomas survived all that, but in May, 1818, he eventually succumbed to persistent heavy rain on a march from Portsmouth to Plymouth. He began to cough up blood, was excused from playing in the Band, and spent two months in hospital. His last letter suggests he might come home to convalesce. Whether he ever did so is uncertain, but he died four months later in November, 1818, in Plymouth, aged thirty-six, a sergeant and a Peninsular veteran. His last letter home contains none of the resentment and antagonism of the earlier letters, and he signs himself 'Your Affectionate Son Thos. Fisher'.

Far though he travelled, Thomas did not get as far as his younger brother, William, who reached Jamaica (Figure 7). William was not an obvious candidate for working in a tropical climate, with his delicate constitution. Thomas, with all the worldliness of an elder brother, told his father pointedly that 'Foreign countrys particularly such as the West Indies where there are so many bad distempers will not suit such Men as them who never experienced any Climes but by a good comfortable fireside'. Nevertheless, William sailed with three local friends on the *Mary* from Liverpool in early May, 1810, landing at Port Maria in Jamaica on July 1st. He was to be a bookkeeper on an estate in Halifax in the north-eastern parish of St Mary.

He hated it immediately, and wrote a long letter home complaining of the horrors of slavery, of the climate, and of the unreasonable demands of his job. Mr Hodgson, the Liverpool agent, had told him that he would enjoy 'a Gentleman's life', but the reality was different. He had to supervise the slaves from 'day-peep', and attend the daily floggings of evildoers. He was one of only three white men on an estate of 150 'blacks and mungrels'. His fellow white men were 'chiefly Scotch and Irish of bad character who had no trades or wish'd for an idle profligate life & and a great many of them deserters from Jails and ships of war'. There was no chance to

Figure 7. An armed brig in the Mersey in 1810, when William Fisher sailed for Jamaica. *Board of Trustees of the National Museums and Galleries on Merseyside (Merseyside Maritime Museum)*

go to church, the nearest place of worship being twenty miles away, and the parson languishing in jail!

William had chosen a bad time to be a planter. Even though the British had ended the transportation of slaves from Africa three years earlier, life on the Jamaican estates had changed little. Resentment amongst the slaves threatened to lead to insurrection, and William was horrified to discover that he was expected to serve in the whites-only militia, ready to put down any rebellion. He hated the food, which consisted of 'a little cold Coffee & a herring, or a little Irish butter like fish-oil', with only occasionally 'a little salt Beef or Pork'. It rained every day 'as if the Clouds was burst so that the roads are wash'd away & new rivers form'd', and he was expected to supervise the slaves outside in all weathers, often for twenty hours out of twenty-four. Nor was there much money to be made, for his first year's salary had already been deducted to pay for the voyage. His letter is long, as well as vivid, and his handwriting becomes more and more disordered as he tries to finish his letter in time to catch the next ship. With his brother's gift for melodrama, he ends:

> I hear of stout young men geting a hearty dinner & being in the grave the same Day, fevers come on as suden as gunshot daily & sweep men form the Earth they dig a hole behind a bush & throw them in ... .

From Thomas's letters, it is clear that William got his wish, and caught the *Mary* in time to return home by the beginning of November. Thomas's fears that his health was not robust enough for the West Indies were justified, for William died only two years later in November, 1812, aged twenty-six.

Joseph's two other sons enjoyed vastly contrasting fortunes. James, born in 1792, followed his father's lead, and went into the woollen business. In 1820, he was making 'large purchases of Wollan Cloths and Spanish Wool', but his career was cut brutally short when he was thrown from his horse at Castletown in the Isle of Man in 1820 (Figure 8), whilst visiting the island with three Yorkshire friends. He had more than £500 on him at the time of his death, and a fashionable wardrobe, including a pair of Wellington boots. He had also left clothes and cash in a trunk at a Liverpool inn. He was twenty-eight, and buried at old Kirk Braddan Church, near Douglas (Figure 9), on 4 October. His funeral expenses are detailed in one letter, with the hat bands costing more than twice as much as the coffin, and the customary bottle of 'Sherry wine' costing more than either.

Joseph, the youngest son, died in London less than a year before

Figure 8. Castletown, Isle of Man, *c.*1820. *Manx Museum and National Trust*

Figure 9. Old Kirk Braddan Churchyard, where James Fisher was buried in 1820.

his father, at the end of 1836. Edward Rooke, a fellow-Yorkshireman, wrote two very formal letters to Joseph senior announcing his death from typhus fever in the Middlesex Hospital. Joseph junior had apparently been in London since at least 1824, and had eked out a living as a part-time messenger and porter with a Covent Garden pawnbroker, Mr Townsend. Although he was obviously had the implicit trust of Mr Townsend, Joseph had never sought to better his lot, and Rooke regrets 'the impropriety of being so indifferent, as to his advancement in Life'. In response to Joseph's enquiry about his son's churchgoing habits, Rooke laments that he 'did not attend, to any place of Religious Worship' but says that Joseph had admitted that his father 'had endeavoured to inculcate very different sentiments in his earlier years'. He remained unmarried, but had retained his Yorkshire friends, and was known as 'York'.

Joseph Fisher's initial lease on Birks Mill ended in 1831, and it may well be that he retired from business about that time. By the time of his death at the age of seventy-nine in November, 1837, both his wives and every one of his eleven children had predeceased him. There are no records of any of his children marrying, and only two, Thomas and Joseph, reached their thirties. Nonetheless, this Almondbury family played its part in the great sweep of local, national, and international events. The time-span of the letters coincides with the 'Romantic' period of Keats, Shelley, and Byron. However, whilst the Fishers had their ambitions, their beliefs, their passions and their resentments, their letters show them too busy coping with the problems created by a harsh world, by each other, and by illness and death, to approach life in any other than a strictly practical way.

Acknowledgements

Mr E W Aubrook, Director of the Ravensknowle Museum in 1958, showed great interest in the Fisher Letters, and I am grateful for the more recent support of John Rumsby, Collections Team Manager at the Kirklees Community History Service. Mr and Mrs Pilling, formerly of Fenay Grange Farm, Almondbury, have been welcoming and informative, an old friend, Michael Whitworth, has advised on textile matters; and I am grateful for the help of Canon Mark Thomas of Almondbury, Major Deedes, Regimental Secretary at the Light Infantry Office in Pontefract, and to staff at the Bank of England Archive, the Merseyside Maritime Museum, the Manx Museum, and Suffolk Libraries and Heritage.

5. FILM-MAKING OVER THREE CENTURIES: JAMES BAMFORTH AND THE FILM-MAKING PIONEERS

by Ian Harlow

HOLMFIRTH IS ONLY A SMALL YORKSHIRE TOWN yet it has a claim to fame as one of the pioneering centres for film making in the world. At the end of the nineteenth century many people from all over the world were trying to capture the illusion of movement in pictures – in America, in France, in Germany and in Yorkshire. Many different systems were being devised to be the first to advance from still photographs to moving pictures.

West Yorkshire can claim to have seen some of the earliest movies, using a British patented camera invented by a French-born man, Louis Aime Augustin Le Prince. Two fragments, dating from November, 1888, are still in existence. The first one was of Le Prince's English father-in-law, Mr Joseph Whitley and was filmed at Roundhay, Leeds, at the rate of ten to twelve frames per second. The second fragment showed traffic moving over Leeds Bridge and was shot at twenty frames per second. The pictures were improving, with the original jerkiness being much smoothed out in the second film. The pictures were so clear that it was claimed that smoke could be seen rising from the pipe of a lounger on the bridge.

Le Prince also provided the film making industry's first, still unsolved, mystery. Following his work in Leeds, he had built a new projector, making use of the new convenience of celluloid roll film instead of the old, cumbersome medium. He was on his way to New York from his home in France to present his new invention to the public for the first time. On 16 September 1890, he boarded the Paris-bound train in Dijon – and was never seen again. He never arrived in Paris and his body was never found. Exhaustive enquiries were made but no rational explanation was found for his disappearance.

The Magic Lantern
Long before that time, however, back in Holmfirth, Mr James Bamforth had noticed the potential of the 'Magic Lantern' and in 1870 founded his own company to advance the educational and entertainment virtues he envisaged. His father was a painter and

decorator and James had an interest in carpentry and the new craft of photography. He also had an imaginative and artistic flair with a genius for presentation, coupled with business acumen.

The magic lantern had been known for some time (Samuel Pepys had observed it in his diary and that was in the seventeenth century) and by 1870 it was an apparatus which was relatively simple to use and could produce clearly defined pictures. James's services were much in demand and he gave illustrated talks, story recitals, popular entertainments and lectures for businesses as far away as Halifax and Wakefield. He gave charity exhibitions for Temperance Societies, Band of Hope meetings, Sunday Schools and other church events, and these were much appreciated.

The technical aspects of the magic lantern, in the days before electricity, were impressive. Two cylinders, one of oxygen and one of hydrogen, were required on site for illumination; they could be a dangerous, not to say lethal, combination. They had to be hauled to each location, which, given the hills which surround Holmfirth, was no easy task. It was at least a two man job.

James Bamforth worked hard at his art. He was the pioneer of many techniques which are today commonplace in the film industry. In particular he developed 'pavilions', in effect film sets, on the slopes near his factory in Holmfirth. These were atmospheric locations, usually with a painted backdrop, which formed the setting for his actors and actresses to pose as 'life models' and illustrate the great themes of his magic lantern shows. The 'pavilions' could be used and adapted over and over again.

He used local people, both adults and children, in his photographs on slides and started, in effect, the 'stars' system. Although technically amateurs, he paid two old pence (about one new penny) for those in the crowd and four old pence (not quite two new pence) for 'starring' roles. Thus whilst taking his photographs he was ensuring that he would have a willing audience, as everyone was eager to see themselves on screen in this novel form of entertainment.

James Bamforth worked on the slides and the story line to create maximum melodramatic effect. The new science of photography was the basis for his slides. His actors and actresses, posing in their pavilions, had to stay very still whilst the photograph was taken. Photospeeds were improving, but nevertheless photographs tended to be very 'wooden'. The pictures were of course in black and white only, so he had the slides painted to create the lifelike impressions that he required. The slides were then mounted in glass to provide great durability. All this, together with a dramatic narrative and

I LOVE A LASSIE (2).

I love a lassie, a bonnie, bonnie lassie,
She's as pure as the lily in the dell,
She's as sweet as the heather, the bonnie
bloomin' heather,
Mary, ma Scotch bluebell.

Figure 1. *I Love a Lassie* – A James Bamforth postcard illustrating a song made famous by Sir Harry Lauder.

sound effects from a harmonium could give an impressive illusion for his audience.

As a businessman he realised that he had to meet the needs of his customers and he was willing to use any suitable theme. One of his favourite ideas was to create a story from the current songs – an early version of *Top of the Pops*. Many Victorian ballads were ideal material for a sequence of illustrations; songs like *The Volunteer Organist*; *My Grandfather's Clock*; *It is Christmas Day in the Workhouse*; *Billy's Rose*; *I Love a Lassie* (Figure 1). He claimed that he was able to create illustrations for any song title within one hour – a very creditable achievement in its day. Eventually he had a stock of over 2,000,000 titles for sale to the general public.

The experience obtained from these techniques became the source of the skills required when moving pictures became possible. James Bamforth started his company in 1870, but it was over twenty years before developments in photography made 'movies' possible. Although magic lantern shows are now considered to be very old fashioned, very Victorian, they were in their day the most modern and hi-tech form of entertainment. James Bamforth fully earned the title given to him by the newspapers – 'King of the Lantern Slides'.

Postcards
James's business was developing on two tracks – magic lantern shows and illustrated cards, which later became postcards. Postcards were invented (although to call them an 'invention' seems to be over pretentious) on the continent. The system of the prepaid 'penny' post was an English idea put forward and implemented by Rowland Hill, in spite of some reluctance by the Post Office. Postcards seemed to be a natural progression from this.

The Post Office view was that correspondence was private and therefore postcards, which anyone could read whilst in transit, were violations of this privacy. However, the use of postcards was suggested in Germany in 1865 and they were finally adopted and issued in Austria in 1869. *Korrespondenz Karte* (as they called them) were an immediate success and within a month a million and a half had been sold. These postcards were simply cards – plain and unillustrated. In time they became the nineteenth century equivalent of the twentieth century telephone, or the twenty-first century e-mail or text message.

By 1894 postcards were accepted in Great Britain, although it was some years later before the key development of **picture** postcards took place. This was the acceptance, in 1902, of space for both a message and the address on one side of the card – leaving the other side for the picture. Germany and France followed this practice in 1905, and the way was open for a boom in the sending of picture postcards. Picture postcards became the mainstay of the Bamforth business over many years. Photographs were the first novelty, but later Edwin Bamforth, James's son, developed the comic illustration, which are now made all over the world. Another First for Holmfirth!

Moving Pictures in the Nineteenth Century

Before this had happened, however, James Bamforth had launched his latest enterprise – moving pictures for public display. He was one of the world's first in this spectacular new industry having, as we have seen, already pioneered many ideas later adopted all over the world.The idea of using moving pictures as entertainment was a natural progression from the dramatic magic lantern shows which he had perfected over the years. The original films were shown as short exhibition acts in the Music Halls.

A company called Riley Brothers from Bradford had acquired a new kinematograph camera and had tentatively started making and showing their 'animated' pictures. James Bamforth saw a demonstration at a Band of Hope meeting in the Victoria Hall in Huddersfield in 1898 and immediately saw the commercial possibilities. The two companies were an ideal match; Riley Brothers had the expertise on the use of the kinematographic camera and James Bamforth the expertise in the production of shows. Together they started a company, called RAB (Riley And Bamforth?) to make moving pictures. It was now a real family business with his children Frank, Edwin, Harry and Janie Bamforth all involved in different capacities.

These were of course silent films, but with action in plenty. The stories were simple, graphic and (usually) comic – real slapstick for the most part. They were short, about five minutes on average, although curiously they are advertised by length of film, in feet. Once more James used local people, amateurs, for his actors and actresses, with an interested crowd to watch this strange new phenomena. He created the screen's first comedian, Fred Beaumont, a French polisher by trade.

A sample of film titles, made in the years 1897 to 1900, give a flavour of the plots used:

> *Watering the Gardener, Pillow Fight, The Runaway Knock and the Suffering Milkman, Weary Willie in the Park, Gossips and Eavesdroppers, The Biter Bit, The Tramp and the Baby's Bottle, Catching the Milk Thief, Leapfrog*

The photographic business and the film making business complemented and supported each other. A postcard 'Wet Paint', with a series of pictures and an explanatory rhyme (Figure 2), illustrated *Weary Willie in the Park. Gossips and Eavesdroppers* (Figure 3) used the same tactics, but used one of the illustrations for the moral of the story – 'Don't talk about your neighbours; if your tongue

Figure 2. *Wet Paint* – a postcard with the story of the film *Weary Willie in the Park*. The individual picture captions recount the story –

A painter at his work is seen,
applying varnish bright and clean.
A masher takes the vacant seat
And hopes his lady love to greet!
He finds he cannot leave his seat
Not even his best girl to greet.
She concludes amidst her sighs,
His love is cold or he would rise.
This is the masher's only mode
Of escaping down the road.
A curious bird drops on the scene
And wonders what the pants have been.

needs exercise, chew gum'. *Bobby's Flirtation* and *Robert on Duty* both illustrate aspects of *The Tramp and the Baby's Bottle*.

The Bamforth company can claim to be one of the earliest businesses in the country to make cinematograph films for public entertainment. They were premiered to appreciative audiences in Holmfirth, who enjoyed seeing themselves and their own home grown stars in action, with contributions from water, snow and custard pies. Since the town was frequently brought to a standstill when some of the films were being made, the finished product was

Figure 3. *Gossips and eavesdrippers* – a postcard with a moral!
"As if we down-trod women hadn't any common rights."
Stood Mr Niggle, listening to what they had to say.
"We'll get their tails in quietly and nail them to the boards."
They fished for and the tails they hooked without the slightest noise.
While Niggle, with his worthy boy, in flight now safety seeks.
And now behold the champions of women's every right.

And the moral of the story is – 'Don't talk about your neighbours; if your
tongue needs exercise, chew gum'.

eagerly awaited. Then, as now, a film or television crew could draw
the crowds and stop the traffic.

Films were shown all over West Yorkshire – Huddersfield, Halifax,
Leeds, Sheffield and as far away as Manchester. Another original
feature which James Bamforth used in his film shows was the sound
effects provided by Thomas Edison's new invention, the
phonograph. He was able to use appropriate stirring music such as
Tommy Atkins, *Soldiers of the Queen* and *The Holy City* to create the
right patriotic atmosphere. This was particularly appropriate for
enlisting support for the Boer War effort.

In 1902 Bamforth's found it necessary to move their premises
from Prickleden into a more central position at Hillside in
Holmfirth. The new premises were purpose built to give plenty of
light for their work in producing slides and picture postcards. It was

at this time that picture postcards came into general use in England and film making, after such a promising start, was suspended for ten years. The Company wished to concentrate on more profitable activities.

Moving Pictures in the Twentieth Century (1)

In 1912 the Valley Theatre was opened on River Walk in the centre of Holmfirth. The Theatre presented theatrical shows and films, not surprisingly since James Bamforth had an interest in the venture. With this impetus Bamforth's started to make films again, with all his experience and enthusiasm and with more up to date equipment. All the old Bamforth skills were evident; in addition he used some professional actors and actresses, recruited locally and from further afield. The films were slightly longer than formerly – eight to eleven minutes being the average (500/700 feet), although some multi-reel films were produced.

More than a hundred films were produced between 1913 and 1915 by Bamforth and Co. and the Holmfirth Production Company. Most of these were comedy films featuring another of the cinema's early comic characters – Winky, an eccentric gentleman who got himself into various scrapes collectively known as *Winky's Misadventures*. Some of the titles gave an indication of these activities – *Winky's Fireworks*; *Winky's Jealousies*; *How Winky fought for a bride*; *Winky and the Gorgonzola Cheese* and *Winky the Bigamist*. Winky was played by Reginald Switz.

A poster illustrating some films called Winky 'The New Picture Comedian' (Figure 4), with Bamforth Films producing 'The freshest and funniest comedies now on the market.' They were being produced, apparently, in about three days. Other productions included 'The Greatest Discovery of British Film History', Baby Langley, 'Without a shadow of doubt The Cleverest Child Picture Player in the World – and she is English.' Again Holmfirth leads the world in the art of hyperbole.

James Bamforth created more stars of the silent screen and all

Figure 4. An advertisement for 'WINKY, the New Picture Comedian'.

Figure 5. The winsome Mary Winterman, one of Holmfirth's first starlets.

clearly very local to Holmfirth – Hannah Hinchliffe, Marion Barrowclough, Mary Winterman (Figure 5), Ingham Hoyle, Edgar Irwin, Haigh Gledhill. He did not use stage names for his stars; he left that to the Americans.

Other films could best be described as romantic or melodramatic. In particular a dramatic film *Paula*, about one and a half hours in duration, featured some of the first nationally known stars like Queenie Thomas – a real heart-throb in her day.

Production continued at a rapid rate until wartime conditions in 1915 made film production too difficult. The films were distributed to many parts of the world and 100 were on order for delivery to Russia in 1915 – but they were never completed. Production of filmmaking was suspended. When production ceased Frank Bamforth opined that 'We were streets ahead of American production methods and techniques'. Production never started again after the war and world leadership passed from Holmfirth to Hollywood (Figure 6).

Just occasionally over the next sixty years film crews came to Holmfirth. In particular a family saga of the fictitious Crowther

Figure 6. The Valley Theatre, Holmfirth, as it was in the 1930s, proudly announcing the latest idea – Talkies! The covered way in front of the cinema was washed away in the 1944 flood.

family *The Master of Bankdam* was made and released in 1947. This nineteenth century Yorkshire epic, illustrating 'trouble at t'Mill' featured some names later well known, (Dennis Price, Jimmy Hanley, David Tomlinson) but did not achieve great distinction.

Moving Pictures in the Twentieth Century (2)

It was in 1972 that film making returned to Holmfirth. It started very inauspiciously. The BBC had commissioned a comedy by up and coming writer Roy Clarke, a Yorkshireman with a deep insight into Yorkshire psyche. The story lines were written round the adventures (or misadventures) of three middle aged men in their second childhood. They had no obvious home ties and could therefore indulge their slightest whim without any restraint from a domestic partner. The series was not immediately successful, but somehow the public began to warm to the three characters. The interplay between the men began to develop. *Last of the Summer Wine* was born.

The three old codgers enjoying their 'Summer Wine' were Bill Owen, playing Compo, Peter Sallis playing Norman Clegg and (initially) Michael Bates playing Blamire. Within the stories they all had their distinct parts. Compo was the work-shy layabout, with an unrequited passion for his next door neighbour, Nora Batty. Compo was the one to do all the dirty work devised for him by Blamire, usually on the basis that his actions would impress Nora. They did, but only rarely.

Norman Clegg was the philosopher of the trio, always ready with the witty phrase as long as he was not required to do anything. The most exciting thing that he ever did was to get married, but he could never understand how that happened. He is a widower now and a moderately restraining influence on the other two.

Blamire was the man of ideas for action – by other people. Michael Bates died after only a few episodes, and his ideas 'role' was carried out by Brian Wilde (as 'Foggy' Dewhirst) or by Michael Aldridge (as Seymour Utterthwaite) and later still by Frank Thornton (as Truly of the Yard). Most of the ideas were dubious in theory and unmanageable in action – and hilarious in the attempted execution.

Further series were commissioned and further characters were introduced or given more prominence. Sid and Ivy at the café; Nora Batty and her henpecked husband Wally, with his pigeons. Later came Edie and Wesley Pegden, the ubiquitous handyman who could make anything that the mind of man (usually Foggy or Seymour) could devise. They had a daughter Glenda, with husband Barry, eternally trying to better themselves. Clegg's next door neighbours, Pearl and Howard and Howard's badly concealed fancy woman, Marina, all added to the characters. All were recognizable people, just like those living down your street.

The external scenes were shot around the town centre, in the streets and ginnels which are a feature of the locality. Sid's Café was a favourite haunt, with Sid and Ivy, the proprietors, providing a backcloth of domestic disharmony of real Yorkshire wit and invective. The local library was another feature until they were ejected for unsocial behaviour. The local park was used and there were an increasing number of moorland beauty spots which they visited. It was the scenic beauty of the area which attracted many people to come and see Holmfirth and has built up tourism in a way which

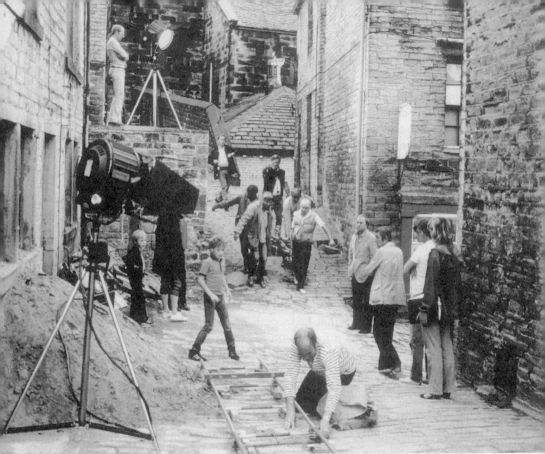

Figure 7. Modern filmmaking requires much more paraphernalia. In Daisy Lane lights have to be arranged and a railway built for moving shots, and there are always spectators!

James Bamforth would certainly have approved (Figure 7).

Year by year more series were produced until it became the world's longest running television comedy show. The public loved it; some people gave their opinion that the television licence was worth the money for that show alone. Clearly there are fanatics who identified themselves with the characters. However, even the younger folk could appreciate the show and there is little in it to cause offence.

Film making for *Last of the Summer Wine* continued for the rest of the twentieth century, and into the twenty-first. It owes its longevity to the way in which the characters were allowed to develop, with the introduction year by year of fresh individuals with their own unique contribution and to the use of backgrounds away from the centre of Holmfirth. There is a practical reason for this. Filming is now a complicated business involving many people. The coachload of back up staff, along with all their equipment, takes up a lot of space and the town centre can be very congested. Other locations nearby had to be used (Figure 8).

Apart from Holmfirth the action is now shared amongst several built up areas, notably Marsden, Jackson Bridge and Hinchliffe Mill. It is still a common sight to see a moorland road suddenly full of film vehicles with their attendant equipment, eating facilities and, of course, a portaloo. And still the filming draws the crowds, even though making a film can be a tedious business. This is especially so for the 'stars' who have to be there for their brief moments of glory, perhaps carried out many times until the director is satisfied with the performance.

Last of the Summer Wine has been in production for such a long time that fiction and fact have became intertwined. Sid's Café is indeed now a café, although Sid has been dead for many years. Nora Batty's wrinkled stockings draw crowds to the 'Wrinkled Stocking Café'. It would be no surprise to come round any corner and come face to face with a character straight out of the show. Bill Owen, who made the part of Compo his own (and has had a café named after him as well) was so happy in Holmfirth that it became his second

Figure 8. Much filming is done in the countryside to avoid inconveniencing too many people. On the right Compo, Foggy and Clegg are having a deep philosophical discussion (probably on wrinkled stockings) whilst the others get everything ready for the next shot.

home. He did indeed walk round the town like any other citizen, although somewhat more nattily dressed than Compo.

The mingling of fact and fiction became even more marked. Bill Owen died whilst a series was being filmed. He had bravely carried on although gravely ill. On his death the series was re-written and his fictional funeral, together with the preparations, became a moving tribute to his life and work. He was buried, as he wished, in the churchyard which looks out over the centre of the town which he had come to love. On his gravestone are a pair of miniature wellies which were his 'trademark'.

Even more remarkably, his real life son Tom was reunited with his father, and *Last of the Summer Wine* continues with his long lost son returning to carry on the family tradition.

Holmfirth and the surrounding areas have been the location for other television films or series. *Where the Heart Is* and *The League of Gentlemen* are two recent series which have used the photogenic properties of the area to good advantage. Some years ago Selwyn Froggatt (Oh! No!) and parts of *In Loving Memory* (and again starring Thora Hird) were filmed nearby. We are already in the twenty-first century and it seems likely that film making will continue to carry on the traditions started by James Bamforth in 1870 with his Magic Lantern.

6. READ HOLLIDAY AND LUNNCLOUGH HALL: A NINETEENTH CENTURY ENTREPRENEUR AND HIS HOME

by David Griffiths

READ HOLLIDAY OF HUDDERSFIELD (1809-89) became the leading British dye manufacturer in the latter part of the nineteenth century. In the mid-1850s he built a 'commodious mansion', Lunnclough Hall, off Kaffir Road in the Upper Edgerton district of Huddersfield, where he lived until the early 1870s, shortly after his retirement. The house stayed in the Holliday family's ownership until 1936, and remains privately occupied today, although now divided into two homes. This essay traces the interwoven history of Read Holliday's family, his business and his Edgerton home.

Read Holliday and his business to the mid-1850s

Read Holliday was born in Bingley on 15 September, 1809. His father, Abraham (1745-1825) was one of three brothers described as 'hard-working Yorkshiremen of very modest means' (Fox, 1987). Abraham first worked as a flour miller in Otley; subsequently as a wool spinner at Eldwick Mill, Bingley; and in later years as a tinner in Bradford.

There is no evidence that Abraham accumulated any significant wealth from these varied occupations, with which to give his four children a start in life. Read, the third of these, first worked in his father's spinning mill but soon moved to the chemical industry, joining a Wakefield manufacturer of 'salammoniac' in 1827. He moved on again in 1830 to set up his own business in Huddersfield. There he rented premises at Tanfield Mill, Leeds Road, next to the town's recently-established gasworks; his landlord, almost inevitably, was the Ramsden Estate, who virtually owned the town.

At that time gas was produced by carbonising coal at relatively low temperatures, a process which yielded large volumes of coal-tar and liquor as by-products. The gas industry itself had no use for these, but Holliday recognised them as cheap raw materials with potential for other uses. Initially he was allowed the annual output of liquor for £5, and the tar for free. It was the first coup for an entrepreneurial opportunism which was both the strength and weakness of the business empire he was to create over the next forty years.

Holliday's initial business was the distillation of ammonia from the liquor. This was sold to the clothing industry as a scouring agent, in place of the traditionally-used 'sig' or stale urine. Soda ash and washing powder were also produced. The business gradually developed through the 1830s, and attracted some nuisance complaints from neighbouring property owners.

Perhaps surprisingly, during these years the young entrepreneur was linked to radical politics. He was a supporter of the Republican Volunteers in 1833, and one of utopian socialist Robert Owen's local followers who founded the Hall of Science in Bath Street in 1838 (Brooke, 1993). In 1839, however, he moved to a larger site at nearby Turnbridge, again leased from the Ramsdens, for both works and home, and married Emma Copley of Hunslet. Whether as a result of his growing business or his family responsibilities, that was also the year of his last recorded connection with the Owenite movement.

In these early years, the coal-tar was used only as a fuel, but in 1845 Holliday began to distill this too, producing naphtha and creosote. The latter found a ready market for treating railway sleepers, as this was the height of 'railway mania'. But the former was more important to Holliday, who obtained his first patent, for a naphtha lamp, in 1848. Holliday's Peerless Lamp was a self-vapourising gas lamp, operating without a wick, and became a household name, winning a premier award at the Great Exhibition of 1851. Tar distillation plants were established in several other towns, plus a London warehouse, and by the late 1850s Holliday's was the largest such business in the north of England.

Meanwhile Holliday and his wife were establishing a large Victorian family. His first son, Thomas, was born in 1840, and by 1855 he had five sons and three daughters. As it grew, the family continued to live within the expanding industrial site, but according to Chadwick (1971), Read formed the view that this was 'not a fit place for eight young children', and in 1853 he decided to move to more salubrious surroundings.

Lunnclough Hall
A Huddersfield man of means, looking for an attractive place to live within easy reach of the town, was likely to turn to Edgerton. This Victorian suburb has 'an inner core of mansion houses which is the largest concentration of big houses to be found in the Huddersfield district' (Brook, 1979). Although the first of these was built around 1820, most of the area only became available for villa development

for the Victorian nouveaux-riche at just the time that Holliday decided to move from Turnbridge. Much of the district, known as Upper Edgerton, was owned by the Thornhills of Fixby Hall, but in 1844, when Thomas Thornhill IV died, his widow remarried and 'decided that Fixby Hall was not a desirable mansion for [their daughters] to live in' (Ahier, 1937). The family moved to Dingley Park, Northamptonshire, and the *Thornhill Estate Acts* of 1852-55 enabled much of the estate, including Upper Edgerton, to be sold off. Typically the sales took the form of 999-year leases and a development boom ensued, although the Estate prepared a master plan for the area and maintained close control of development.

Read Holliday's lease ran from 1 November 1854, initially covering 5,700 square yards at a ground rent of £28 per annum (three further plots were added in 1868 to bring the total holding to 8,060 square yards). The site was to the north of Halifax Road, off what became Kaffir Road. The cost of the new home is not known, but Holliday financed its construction by selling off one of his tar distilleries, and took up residence in 1855.

From 1855 to 1859, Holliday was under sustained pressure from the Improvement Commissioners – forerunners of Huddersfield Corporation – to abate the noxiousness of his operations at Turnbridge. Although part of the works was moved to Dalton in 1857, nearer to the River Colne and further from the built-up town, this did not end the criticisms, and in frustration Holliday threatened in 1860 to leave Huddersfield and continue his operations elsewhere. At this point it seems that an accommodation was reached and hostilities called off – but not before Holliday had instructed estate agents to offer Lunnclough Hall for auction. As a result, detailed sale particulars were drawn up when the house was only five years old, and presumably still very much in its pristine state. These paint a splendid picture, not only of the house itself, but of the social and personal meanings of its style and location.

The Victorian architectural 'battle of the styles' was just beginning, and the builders of Edgerton adopted a rich profusion of Gothic, Italianate, Neo-Classical and other less identifiable styles. The sale particulars are headed:

Handsome Suburban Residence In the Pointed Gothic Style of Architecture, which will be offered for Public Competition, by Mr Eddison.

Then comes the opening peroration to several thousand words of detail:

Lunnclough Hall is a New and Elegant Mansion, beautifully situated at Edgerton, 'the Belgravia of Huddersfield', a convenient distance from the town; it is built upon an eminence, completely detached, and surrounded with scenery of an undulating character; the Lawn extends to the three fronts, and a magnificent belt of full grown Oak, Ash and Elm Trees, brings out the fine lines of the style in which the House is built ..... This villa is undoubtedly one of the finest specimens of the Gothic, or pointed style of architecture, in this country. Although the whole composition evinces unity of feeling, there is as much variety of feature as we ever remember to have seen introduced successfully in a villa; indeed, perhaps a greater variety of windows, gables and buttresses than could be introduced in a building of that size with good effect, were it not supported by the corresponding intricacy and variety of the trees around it, which are here in admirable keeping with the picturesque outlines of the edifice.....

It is approached from the Halifax Road, the distance from which is 120 yards, thus getting clear of the dust, and numerous annoyances of the Highway. It is magnificently grand in all its proportions, inside as well as outside; and is a proper residence for a Merchant Prince, who can retire from the busy hum and turmoil of active life into this his quiet home, nested amidst nature's choicest products... .

There is a great variety of surface, caused by the undulations of the ground, and advantage has been taken of this circumstance to cause the grounds to appear of large extent.

In stressing seclusion, picturesqueness, and the appearance of grandiloquence, this description plays well on many of the architectural and social themes identified in Sheeran's account of the 'brass castles' of the newly-rich Victorian entrepreneurs (Sheeran,1993).

In his family history, Chadwick (1971) attributed the design of the house to John Kirk, a well-known mid-century Huddersfield architect (responsible, for example, for Ebor Mount on nearby New North Rd, and much of Wilshaw Village). However, the original drawings reveal the designer as the more celebrated Pritchett & Son. James Pigott Pritchett (1789-1868) – 'Pritchett of York' – joined Charles Watson in his practice in York in 1813, and set up his own firm there in 1831. He is best-known in Huddersfield for the Palladian railway station (1846-50), and it was in the mid-1840s that the Huddersfield branch office known as Pritchett & Son was established (in fact all three of Pritchett's sons worked in the practice

Figure 1. The carriage porch at Lunnclough Hall.

at some time).

Although generally thought to have done his best work, including the station, in Classical styles, there is a recognised 'Tudor Gothic' strand in his work (Broadbent, 1956). This seems to have found clear expression at Lunnclough Hall, with its hood moulds over the windows, massed chimney stacks and above all the projecting carriage porch, fifteen feet square and formed of three Tudor arches, which is now a listed structure (Figure 1). His nearby Huddersfield College School (1839-40) in New North Road, now part of the Technical College, although larger is very similar in its detailing. However, we cannot be sure whether Lunnclough was in fact the work of Pritchett himself, or one of the sons.

From a distance the most striking external feature of the house is the octagonal crenellated tower, described by Eddison's as the

Figure 2. The sixty-foot campanile.

'campanile' (Figure 2). This is sixty feet high, with sweeping views in all directions, reached by a spiral staircase from the second floor of the house. The 1860 particulars describe it as an 'observatory' and comment:

> ...*six people can sit in it comfortably. Gentlemen fond of the weed can enjoy themselves to perfection in this airy region. Four of the windows open for the purpose of using telescopes.*

The freely-designed Gothic exterior is, however, a façade for a basically symmetrical interior – a juxtaposition which would certainly have offended purists of the Gothic Revival such as John Ruskin. The

Figure 3. The top-lit dome above the hall.

dominant interior feature is a circular hall, some 16 feet in diameter. Top-lit through a painted dome, which is enclosed within a gabled roof and thus invisible from outside (Figure 3), this gives rise to a very distinctive ground floor plan (Figure 4), with the principal

Figure 4. The ground-floor plan, with the principal rooms surrounding the circular hall.

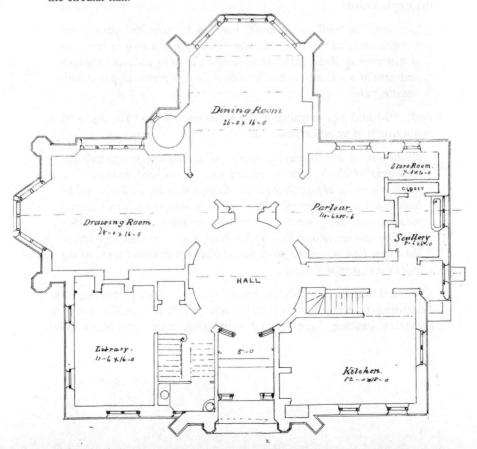

rooms, staircase and kitchen corridor radiating from the circular central lobby. The drawing room, dining room and breakfast room were linked by pairs of double doors. The resulting direct access from drawing room to dining room presumably precluded any opportunity to lead dinner guests through the impressive hall, contravening one rule of Victorian good taste (Sheeran, 1993), but had other advantages, as the 1860 sale particulars explained:

> *While any portion of the house may by itself be used by the family at any time, the effect of the entire first floor, when thrown open at once, would be more striking than that of many mansions we have seen of four times the size, where the rooms, having no connexion, and being badly arranged, produced little effect as a whole.*

Once again, as with the grounds, here is the emphasis on a 'trompe l'oeil' enlargement of what is in reality a quite compact villa.

On the first floor were five bedrooms, two with attached dressing rooms, and a bathroom, leading off a landing which circled the hall behind an iron balustrade. On the second floor were three further bedrooms, one described as the 'servants' bedroom' and another as the 'governess' bedroom'. If the servants' accommodation was limited, the sale particulars give one part of the explanation:

> *...it may be well to mention here that there are nine fixed washstands ... in the house, therefore, there is no fetching or carrying of water up or down stairs, thus saving the most valuable strength and time of a servant, indeed enabling the occupier to dispense with one altogether.*

Both cold and hot running water were on tap, and the agent also made much of another 'mod con':

> *All the rooms are thoroughly ventilated, there being two ventilation flues, into which the vapours arising from gas or other matters pass, through horizontal pipes fixed in the ceilings, 6 inches in diameter. The bedrooms are also thoroughly provided for in this particularly essential manner, there being ventilating draughts up the buttresses, and lofers over the door-ways into the circular Hall; and to prevent any failure the owner had one of the justly famed Watson's ventilators, out of the roof of the circular hall....*

Watson, it may be recalled, had been Pritchett's early partner in York. According to Broadbent (1956), such practical considerations as acoustics, heating, lighting and ventilation 'were Pritchett's chief delight'. He and Watson provided for a particularly complex system at the Wakefield Pauper Lunatic Asylum (1816-18), while Pritchett's arrangements at Huddersfield College School were almost as elaborate.

The Holliday business after 1860

After his decision to stay in Huddersfield, Read Holliday led his business into the new field for which it became best-known. Until 1856, dyestuffs were made from plants such as madder and indigo. In that year, however, the great British chemist W H Perkin first successfully manufactured aniline (synthetic) dyes from coal tar, and Hollidays lost little time in seizing this new business opportunity, first producing Magenta in 1860 or 1861. The shift to dyestuffs was timely, as paraffin was now threatening the market for naphtha lamps.

However, from 1861-65 Holliday had to fight a major legal battle against Messrs Simpson, Maule & Nicholson, who claimed Holliday's new products infringed earlier and more generalised patents of their own. Holliday eventually won, albeit at great cost, in the House of Lords, and thus 'set free the entire aniline colour-making industry' (Chadwick, 1971). The official historian of ICI – of which, as we shall see, Hollidays was a forerunner – has explained why this opened up a dynamic period of growth for British dyestuffs:

> ...if there was one country above all others that might have been expected to become the headquarters of synthetic dyes, that country was England. There seemed every reason why this should be so. First, the demand: Great Britain had the world's largest textile industry. Next, the first great discovery – Perkin's – had been made in England, and Perkin was no unworldly scholar unaware of the commercial possibilities of what he had done... Thirdly, the essential raw material for aniline and other anthracene dyes – coal – was what Great Britain possessed an almost inexhaustible supply of. Moreover a great deal of gas was made in Great Britain, yielding coal-tar as a by-product. (Reader, 1970.)

The strategic opportunities for the new technology were, of course, exactly those on which Holliday had based his original business thirty years before. The firm went on to make a wide range of dyestuffs, including Spirit Blue, Basic Green and many others as well as the original Magenta, plus raw materials such as nitrobenzene, aniline and toluidine for other dye-makers, and came to dominate dyestuffs as they had tar distilling earlier.

Read Holliday retired in 1868, leaving his sons to manage the business, but remained at Lunnclough Hall. He served briefly on the newly-formed Huddersfield Corporation in 1868-69, but found politics uncongenial, and retreated to Harrogate in the early 1870s. Lunnclough Hall had given him a taste for house-building: he had built and under-leased three more houses in Kaffir Road during the 1860s, and continued to build during his later years in Queen's Road, Harrogate.

Lunnclough Hall was once again put on the market in 1874, but again went unsold. It was at about this time, though, that Read's eldest son Thomas (1840-98), now the senior partner and general manager of the business, married, and the house became home to him, his wife Maria (1854/5-1935/6) and, in due course, their three children.

Apart from his house-building hobby, it seems that Read had been very much driven by the needs of the business, with little time for public life. Although Thomas made a major technical as well as managerial contribution to the firm, obtaining twenty-nine patents between 1863 and his death in 1898, he also found more time to contribute to the life of the town. He was a keen sportsman, serving as life president of the Huddersfield Cricket & Athletics Club and president of the Huddersfield Chess Club; active in politics as a Liberal (later Liberal Unionist); a director of the West Riding Union Bank; and eventually a JP.

Neither Read nor Thomas maintained an ostentatious household at Lunnclough Hall. The Census records a governess and two house servants in 1861; a cook/domestic servant and a general domestic servant in 1871; a nurse, cook and housemaid in 1881, when Thomas's children were very young; and a governess, cook and two housemaids in 1891. This – the largest recorded domestic establishment – may well have reflected a time of particular prosperity for Thomas and his family. Read Holliday had died in 1889 (and is buried at Edgerton Cemetery, half a mile from Lunnclough Hall), leaving a personal estate valued at £19,099 11s 1d gross (£18,803 net). While this seems a remarkably modest sum, perhaps understated by 'death-bed gifts', applying a general price deflator it would still equate to £500-600,000 today. Moreover, the greater part of the estate took the form of domestic property – the four houses in Edgerton and no fewer than seven by this time in Harrogate, with other property in Blackburn and London (Holliday, 1889). Given the long-run tendency for property prices to inflate with earnings rather than general prices, it is probably realistic to regard Read Holliday, at his death, as a personal millionaire in today's terms.

At the same time the business was valued at £58,000. At this point the sons chose to 'go public', and a limited company was established in 1890 with a capitalisation of £200,000. The Turnbridge site by this time covered 14 acres, and in 1897 there were 15 distinct laboratories there, and 1,500 employees. But industrial storm-clouds were gathering:

> *During the period 1886-1900 the six largest German firms completed 948 British patents. The six largest English firms together completed only 84, of which Read Holliday took the lead with 28, a smaller total than the smallest of the German firms under consideration.* (Holme, 1988)

For the five Holliday brothers, in any event, the good times were short-lived. Edgar, who managed the New York branch established in 1864, died in 1891; Charles, who was Thomas's chief assistant in the business, in 1893; John, a product chemist and later a debt-ridden 'black sheep', in 1894; Thomas in 1898; and Robert, another technical innovator, manager of the Wakefield branch and chairman after Thomas's death, in 1901. All five had died in their forties and fifties, and many attributed this to the effects of their early upbringing at Turnbridge (though Robert was born at Lunnclough Hall) – perhaps the Improvement Commissioners had been right after all!

This family devastation coincided with a low point for the business, with C M Whittaker, joining the firm in 1899, finding it in a state of near-bankruptcy (Whittell, 1984). Reader (1970) sees this as the consequence of the firm's tradition of industrial opportunism, pitted against the German scientific and technical standards of their Manchester competitors, Levinstein's. Read Holliday, he writes:

> *...had none of the solid basis provided by German connections, but on the other hand they were quick to recognise profit in specific processes... Some of their products were bluntly described by... Whittaker as 'fakes', by which he meant that they met their customers' needs by mixing dyes already on their list and sometimes adding imported dyes made by the German competitors... Opportunism tinged with rascality was hardly so strong a foundation for an allegedly science-based business, as the immense chemical expertise of the Germans, or even of Levinstein Ltd.*

The brothers' deaths left the company without a Holliday in its leadership for some months in 1901, but in October of that year Thomas's son Lionel (L B Holliday), born at Lunnclough Hall in 1880, joined the board, becoming chairman in 1908, with Joseph Turner as an admired general manager. The firm enjoyed revived profits over these years, partly on the back of demand for Boer War uniforms and Japanese army blankets.

The outbreak of the First World War cut British textile-makers off from German supplies and focused official attention on the weakness of the domestic dyestuffs industry. Partly to address this immediate problem, and partly with an eye to post-war competitive strength, the Government and textile industry developed proposals to merge several businesses as British Dyes Ltd. The new firm

> *...were determined to have Read Holliday – it was one of the specific reasons for founding the company – and they had no great difficulty in coming to terms, no doubt because the terms they offered were extremely attractive... On 1 July, 1915 British Dyes paid out £537,000 to the owners of Read Holliday, and £10,000 each to Major L.B.Holliday, then at the war, and Joseph Turner.* (Reader, 1970.)

Conclusion

As an archetypal tale of Victorian entrepreneurship, the story of Read Holliday and Lunnclough Hall is almost too good to be true.

On the business side, Read's family background was one of 'very modest means'. He built up a thriving business in a succession of new fields, by dint of commercial opportunism and technical inventiveness, and passed it on to his sons in a seemingly vigorous state. But in fact the business was already losing ground, as new English industries so often did, to more scientifically-based German competition, and eventually survived only by virtue of state intervention.

Meanwhile, after twenty-five years of effort Read had accumulated sufficient capital to move to an arcadian retreat, albeit within easy reach of the works. Within its romantic setting, as we have seen, both house and garden were consciously designed to belie their compactness and emulate a grander scale of country living. As master of the house, Thomas found time, where Read had not, to engage in a range of civic and charitable pursuits, as well as attending to the immediate needs of the business. There was even a wayward son, an indebted and disinherited 'black sheep', to complete this Victorian novel-for-real.

Postscript

In 1914 Eddison's once again drew up sale particulars for Lunnclough Hall, which was 'in the occupation of Mrs Holliday, who is leaving the town'. Additional amenities by this time included a tennis court, summerhouse and radiators in the principal rooms. Yet again, however, the sale did not take place, and the electoral register for 1935 shows Maria Holliday, Thomas's widow, still resident. But a hand-written addition indicates her death, and in 1936 the lease passed from the Trustees of Thomas Holliday to Herbert William Hirst, a local mill-owner.

British Dyes Ltd was not a success, and was subject to further Government-sponsored mergers, first with the old rival Levinstein's to create the British Dyestuffs Corporation in 1919, and then with other chemical industry giants to form ICI in 1926. Their site at Dalton – now occupied by Syngenta and Avecia following ICI's demerger and subsequent restructuring – is the lineal descendant of Read Holliday's original business. And until very recently, the Holliday name lived on too, right next door at Deighton. It was there that Lionel Holliday used the proceeds from the 1915 buy-out to establish his own business, L B Holliday & Co Ltd, often in direct rivalry with its predecessor. He lived until 1967, and Holliday Chemical Holdings stayed in business until February 2001, when new owners Yule Catto decided to close the business. As this book goes to press, the Holliday site is up for sale, and its industrial future unknown.

Acknowledgements

An earlier version of this article appeared in 'Yorkshire History Quarterly', vol 3, no 2, November 1997. Permission to reproduce material from there is gratefully acknowledged.

The major sources for Holliday's life are Fox (1987) and Chadwick (1971). Fox is largely concerned with the industrial history, but draws on Chadwick for domestic and family detail. Some further information is added by Holme (1988), Jenkins (1992) and Whittell (1984). I have drawn on all these sources as well as my own research.

I am most grateful to Mr & Mrs Woods, the present owners of the larger part of the house, for allowing me to visit their home and for lending me papers and photographs; to Mr and Mrs McNeill, whose modern home is on the site of Lunnclough Hall's tennis courts, for allowing me access to papers; and to Messrs Carter Jonas of Slaithwaite, present-day agents of Thornhill Yorkshire Estates, for allowing me to inspect and copy the architect's drawings and plans.

Sources

Ahier, Philip, 'Story of the Manor of Fixby and its Lords', *Huddersfield Weekly Examiner*, 16/1/37.
Broadbent, G H, 'The life and work of Pritchett of York', in W A Singleton (ed), *Studies in Architectural History*, vol.ii, London, 1956.
Brook, J C, *The Development of the Edgerton District of Huddersfield during the 19th Century – with*

Particular Reference to the People who Lived There, mimeo, Huddersfield, 1979.

Brooke, A, *The Hall of Science: Co-operation and Socialism in Huddersfield c. 1830-1848*, Honley, 1993.

Chadwick, Stanley, 'The Read Holliday Story', *Huddersfield Weekly Examiner*, 4/9/71, 11/9/71, 18/9/71, 25/9/71, 2/10/71.

Fox, M R, *Dye-Makers of Great Britain, 1856-1976: a History of Chemists, Companies, Products and Changes*, Manchester, 1987.

Holliday, Read, Will, 1889 – held at West Yorkshire Archives Service, Wakefield.

Holme, Ian, *A Centenary History of the Dyeing and Finishing Industry: Huddersfield Region*, Bradford, 1988.

Jenkins, David T, 'Textiles and Other Industries, 1851-1914', in E A H Haigh (ed), *Huddersfield: A Most Handsome Town*, Huddersfield, 1992.

Reader, W J, *Imperial Chemical Industries: A History. Vol. 1: The Forerunners 1870-1926*, London, 1970.

Sheeran, George, *Brass Castles: West Yorkshire New Rich and their Houses, 1800-1914*, Halifax, 1993.

Whittell, J F I, 'Read Holliday & Sons', *Huddersfield Local History Workshop Newsletter*, 2, 1984.

7. 'THE FORGOTTEN PEOPLE OF HUDDERSFIELD': CITIZENS OF THE POLISH COMMUNITY

by Stephen Wade

The Polish people who settled in Britain during and immediately after the Second World War have been notable for many things: their contribution to the fight against Hitler; their hard application to work; their love of family life, and perhaps most of all, their condition as people on the margins when we tend to think of immigrants in general.

A conversation with a Polish person provides an instant reminder of the troubled history of their nation. A glance at the history books confirms exactly what upheavals there have been. The notable facts of modern history for Poland have been concerned with pain and suffering: the mass grave at Katyn forest, where 10,000 Polish officers were killed by Russians; the concentration camps; the shifting borders, and the struggle for independence. But there is plenty to celebrate also: the Polish servicemen who fought with Wladyslaw Anders in the Second World War for instance. One of my informants spoke of Poles as 'the forgotten people' and it does seem true that their self-identity has been asserted only quietly, going on unnoticed in perfunctory but confident, meaningful ways within English culture.

The imprint is there in thousands of photograph albums: young men in uniform, some of them fighter pilots, and some veterans of Monte Casino. In Lincolnshire, for instance, several lines of graves mark the place where a dozen or more Polish pilots lie. But how do we usually think of the Polish Britons now? Traditionally, they have been active in organising their own social events and in maintaining their cultural traditions. In Huddersfield, they have quietly got on with life. In fact, as features in the *Examiner* show clearly, they have only been noticeable at a few times of crisis, such as on the visit of Marshall Bulganin and Nikita Kruschev to England in April, 1956, when the *Examiner* noted that over 500 people took part in an organised protest against this official visit.

On that occasion, St Patrick's Roman Catholic Church was 'full to capacity'. Captain Rubash-Pobulinski, who was secretary of the Polish White Cross Organisation in Britain, pointed out that there were two million Poles in Russia, and that Russia should 'withdraw their armies from Poland, and release the Poles who were prisoners in labour camps.'[1]

We are talking about a community which has gradually been eroded as younger people are of course assimilated as British, with their Polish identity gradually receding. But it seems the right time now to ask some questions about this, as it is almost twenty years since the interviewers of the Kirklees Sound Archive questioned a group of Poles in Huddersfield who had been mostly the generation born in the 1920s. The general story of those interviews is a sad one of war, exile, arrival in a strange country, feeling like an outsider, and living in poverty until there is a gradual emergence (usually in the next generation) into 'feeling more like an English person.'

A typical profile in the context of Huddersfield is in the memories of one person in particular who arrived first in Barnsley at Cannon Hall, as part of a Polish Resettlement Corps, and then finding work in a mill in Honley. The voice from that tape is hesitant, struggling to find the fluency in English as it deals with a traumatic past:

Er, it was with an English family. We have a small room which was four of us crammed in it... er accommodation wasn't very good, mind

Figure 1. Our Lady of Czestochowa, Fitzwilliam Street, Huddersfield.

you, housing situation in England wasn't very good either, but it was
a roof over our heads, that was it... [2]

An interesting way to look more closely at the experience of the
Polish community in Huddersfield is to tell the stories of three
people across the generations up to the current parents of the
youngest Poles. It would be possible simply to talk about the church
and the Polish Club, the cultural activities and so on, but looking at
the lives of three people who are part of this larger history will bring
home the truth of the experience with some force. The community
set up a Saturday School and social centre in 1948, and they
appointed their own parish priest in 1949. The church of Our Lady
of Czestochowa was opened in 1962 (Figure 1). But between the
1940s and the present there have been all kinds of comings and
goings: some people have been here from the beginning and some
are late arrivals, but they all play a part in the story of Huddersfield.

Jan Tyminski
Jan (now 'John') was deported from the Soviet Union in the 1940s.
He is a strong, square-set man with a firm jaw-line and a mixture of
gentleness and resolve in his countenance, now seventy five years
old. It is easy to see that he has seen some hardship, but his sense of
humour is joyous. Jan's story perhaps starts with his father, who was
a volunteer in the medical corps in the Great War, and was arrested
in 1939 and deported to Russia, with Jan. Jan then became one of
the Army Apprentices, boy soldiers who were evacuated through the
Middle East and then to Italy. Jan became a signalman in this period
of his life.

When he came to Britain, he was first in Barnsley, working in
textiles, then came to Huddersfield in 1947. He never used his real
skills – as a cartographer – as his eyesight was poor. But he worked
for decades, in engineering and in textiles. He has been active in the
Polish community, and as he had learned English in his military life,
he helped other Poles with their English, such as filling in official
forms.

Jan talks with pleasure about the Polish traditions. He mentions in
particular Christmas Eve: 'like the Scottish New year for us' he says
with a smile. He explains about the importance of seeing the first star
on that night, and then eating twelve different foods. He talks about
breaking bread and sharing it, and the good wishes to one's friends.
He points out that Poland is seventy-five per cent rural, and that it is
no surprise that on the Christmas occasion, there is hay under the

tablecloth, and that traditionally, the people sing both carols and other secular pastoral songs.

It is clear how this memory relates to the larger historical picture; as Neal Ascherson has said about rural life in Poland, throughout the Stalinist period to the rule of Gierek and beyond,

> Life for the peasant was tough. It meant toil from dawn to dusk, on thin medieval strips of land often miles apart. Tractors were rare, usually the privilege of big state farms. The private peasant relied on his blond-maned chestnut horse which pulled the plough and trotted the family cart to mass on Sundays.[3]

Jan's mother died in Russia, and his father was in a camp until the post-Yalta releases. His sister and brother brought the father to England. He has never married, and spends much of his time reading and reflecting. Jan is full of sayings and homely wisdom. He talks about his reading: 'When a part is not used, atrophy sets in.' He relishes talk about the history of Poland, and explains about the changes in the borders in the twentieth century. He relates the irony of both frontiers moving west after Yalta in 1945. Another of his maxims is about the difficulties of trusting people in the past, and says: 'Everybody had the white teeth!' He means that smiles were not genuine back in the hard days at home. But he adds that in history, 'the wheel is round, and as it turns, everyone has a go at being crushed!'

Jan's story, told with wit and wryness, exhibits that reliance on memory and the sense of division in Polish identity, expressed so well by the Polish poet, Czeslaw Milosz, who wants the 'real' history to be told:

> And should not the young generations of the West, if they study history at all, hear about 200, 000 people killed in 1944 in Warsaw, a city sentenced to annihilation by those two accomplices (Hitler and Stalin)[4]

Anna Benbow (nee Kuszczak)

Anna's family settled originally in Rochdale, but she was born in Elblag. She was only eight years old when she came to England, arriving with her parents and five sisters and one brother (Figure 2). Her father, an agricultural manager, saw no future in Poland. During the war he had been captured and taken to Siberia, but was freed thanks to the efforts of General Sikorski, whose picture was permanently on the wall at home after that (Figure 3).

Anna came to Huddersfield in 1993, after her second marriage.

Figure 2. Anna with her family (Anna, on the right, bottom row.

Figure 3. Andrej Koszczak.

Her background is unusual in that her father was Orthodox rather that Roman Catholic. But she considers her story to be typical of her generation. She still feels a strong sense of Polish identity. She talks with vivacity and pleasure about the dances and meetings held in Polish social centres, but her real affections in terms of her Polish

Figure 4. Uncle Alexander and Aunt Marisja.

identity are rooted in the European past, of course. Her fondest memories are of spending time with her uncle and aunt, Alexander and Marisya, on their farm in Paslenk, northern Poland (Figure 4).

The question about what may be seen as really typical Polish, Anna sees as being represented in these people: they were 'poor country people'; they, like so many, returned to their farms after the war but were only allowed to have an income – never to own land. Anna paints a picture of this life; she remembers the fun she had in the barn and the orchard, happy with simple things. She recalls watching her aunt sewing, and notes that typical clothes were thick felt wellington boots and jumpers. The photograph of these good people shows the plaits, plain clothes and dignity of 'hard-working poor people'.

There is no doubt that these qualities have been apparent in the Poles who have become British or who have adapted to life here through sheer industry and perseverance. Anna perhaps sums up one of the

Figure 5. Anna's class at the village school in Paslenk. (She is second from the right, bottom row).

commonest problems on arrival here: the language barrier. She says, 'I was a real scholar in Poland and in England what hit me the hardest was not being able to speak. In Poland I couldn't wait to get home – to books and stories.' She recalls the village school with pleasure, stressing that there was a class in the morning and then a second, for older pupils, in the afternoon (Figure 5).

Like Jan, Anna has built a new life and a fresh sense of herself, but her Polish nature is deep and continues to be a source of strength and pride (Figure 6).

Helen Roberts (née Piwowarski)
Another very typical family story is exemplified by the life of Helen Roberts, a guider in Huddersfield,

Figure 6. Anna at work at the University of Huddersfield.

leading a busy life with her family, and her eighty-four-year-old father, Jozef. Jozef, a member of the Polish Free Army, fought at Monte Cassino, was a prisoner in a concentration camp, and eventually settled in the area, working in the textile industry. All his four brothers have now died, but he has associations still with the homeland, and Helen has been back to Gorzow with him.

Helen talks about her affection for Poland, and like Anna, she recalls the rural community with affection. The most interesting aspect of this is her description of contemporary Poland: she paints a picture of long journeys by bus, kiosks in the streets selling everything from chocolate to soap, and people surviving by sheer enterprise, such as picking mushrooms in the forest and then selling them by the roadside. She points to one difference between Britain and Poland very pointedly when she notes that her son mentioned the graffiti everywhere in Poland. 'Ah but here it is modern art' she was told.

Helen went to Poland in 1966, when she was only eight years old. She may not have realised it at the time, but then, in Gomulka's Poland, things were grim; one historian has said in the later 1960s 'the 'disillusion' catchword had been replaced by 'stagnation' and this in a 'bleak landscape.'[5] Yet, Helen's allegiances to her homeland are not related to this: more to the idyllic and simple life on the land.

Helen has clear memories of life in the Huddersfield Polish community when she was young. In particular, she recalls a trip to an old army barracks in Wales which had been bought by the Polish people in Britain for summer camps. Helen won an award in her *zuche*

Figure 7. Helen Roberts and her family on holiday at the seaside in Mienzedroje.

group (similar to Brownies) and obviously loved the free holiday. She also remembers the language classes, and is proud that she can get by in Polish when visiting the mother country (Figure 7). The classes in Huddersfield were in rooms under the church in Fitzwilliam Street.

Polish people in Huddersfield have obviously played a major part in the industrial history of the area, and their cultural life has also been rich and diverse. Yet, one still has the feeling that the wounds of modern European history have cut deep, and to be Polish in Britain means that you inevitably feel the suffering of this. Yet, as I discovered in learning about the community through these representatives, there is a love of learning, a profound pride, and an amazing ability to adapt and survive in the Polish character. Surely it is time that the archives were up-dated, as a crucial part of local history is still being eclipsed. There is much more to Polish history and the Polish diaspora than the merely retrospective view (important though that is) and the ceremonial cross, erected outside the Polish Roman Catholic Church to commemorate the Holy Year of 1950, should symbolise some kind of renewal, as our culture celebrates its multi-cultural richness and vibrancy.

Acknowledgement

Many thanks to Anna Benbow and Helen Roberts for permission to use their family photographs.

Notes and References

1. See *The Huddersfield Daily Examiner*, 23 April 1956.
2. Kirklees Sound Archives: interview (anonymous interviewee) by M Cybulski, 1985.
3. Neal Ascherson, *The Struggles for Poland* (Michael Joseph, 1987) p189.
4. Czeslaw Milosz, *Nobel Lecture* (Farrar Strauss, Giroux, 1980) p18.
5. Neal Ascherson, see note 3, p174.

8. HUDDERSFIELD PICTURE PALACES PRESENT: 'QUEUING FOR DREAMS'

by Robert Preedy

WHAT FOND MEMORIES! The Princess, Empire, Tudor, Majestic, Star, Grand, Plaza and Ritz. Not forgetting Tom Mix and Pearl White and their twenty weeks of cliffhanging suspense. Such was the popularity of films in Huddersfield that the town once supported twenty-seven cinemas.

When the Ritz opened in 1936 the country was in the middle of turbulent political and social change. The Wall Street crash of 1929 heralded a worldwide slowdown which by 1931 was creating severe difficulties throughout Europe. Here a run on the pound, a balance of payments deficit, a loss of the gold standard and internal Labour Party conflict led to a devastating election in October which reduced their seats in the Commons to just fifty-two.

Unemployment continued to rise throughout the thirties to three million and this, the so called 'devil's decade', was characterized by historians as 'rule by pygmies' – politicians incapable of dealing with the immense social challenges. During this bleak period ordinary working people needed an escape. Stanley Baldwin's rustic images of the 20s – the sound of the scythe against the whetstone, the tinkle of the hammer on the anvil, and the sight of a plough team over the brow of the hill – were fast disappearing. The new reality possibly created the urban ills of today. No wonder entertainment enterprises became so powerful during the prelude to the Second World War.

The decade also saw the birth of popular wireless programmes, but the BBC struggled against the more down to earth output of Radio Luxembourg. Theatres and Music Halls were still hugely popular and often provided radio with their major star comedians and band leaders. But it was the cinema that really captured people's attention with the glamorous images of romance and dance. Mass circulation magazines relayed the showbusiness stories from Pinewood and Elstree, and of course Hollywood. Local newspapers provided daily columns dedicated to film news and gossip. This combination of harsh times, unceasing publicity and the appearance of sound and glorious Technicolor, fueled the boom in cinema attendances.

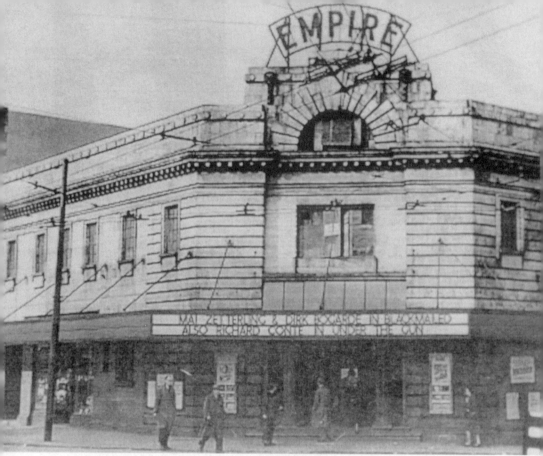

Figure 1. This picture taken in the 1950s shows the Empire in its heyday. Already thirty-five years old by then, it still exuded excitement. By the mid-1980s though, stripped of its sign and canopy it presented a sorry sight in its final guise as an adult film club. *Tony Moss collection*

Major movie chains, mostly financed from America, began a nonstop building programme of supercinemas offering the perfect viewing atmosphere for the 1930s Busby Berkeley fantasies. Losing favour with audiences were the older and functional fleapits which closed during the expensive changeover to sound. The 1930s were a decade of consolidation in the cinema business. The supercinemas were able to gain extended periods of exclusivity, thereby slowing down the supply of film prints to the suburban halls (Figure 1).

When Huddersfield's final centre cinema, the Tudor, closed it ended an incredible entertainment history dating back to the mid nineteenth century. Over the decades the Tudor, in Ramsden Street, had many names and purposes. Originally it opened at a cost of £2,400 on 21 February 1848 as a public riding school. The opening show was by Batty's Circus and theatrical shows became regular attractions. In 1862 the hall was purchased by the 6th West Yorkshire Rifles for use by the Huddersfield Volunteers as a drill hall and armoury. Then for a short time from 1880 theatre returned to the Armoury and by 1900 occasional animated films started to appear, the first on 20 March, *The Transvaal War Day by Day*.

Another change of ownership came within a couple of years when the Northern Theatre Co. Ltd. reopened with the pantomime *Cinderella*. In another name change the Armoury became the Hippodrome when Miss Vesta Tilley opened the entrance with a gold key – the date 21 July 1905. Theatrical shows were supplemented with week long runs of major films like *Birth of a Nation*. Then, from 1926, modernization took place, christening the building the 'New Hippodrome and Opera House'. Within four years films dominated the centre when the Tudor House Super Cinema was born. The opening film (6 October 1930) was *Sons of the Gods*. Throughout this depressed decade many heartwarming and uplifting films were screened such as *King Kong, Anna Karenina,* Disney's *Snow White, Pinocchio* and *Peter Pan,* plus the Pearl White classic thriller starring Betty Hutton, *The Perils of Pauline*.

The year 1950 saw another change of ownership as the Tudor and the nearby Picture House were sold at auction to the Essoldo chain. Fire ravaged the hall in December 1967 but was quickly rebuilt by the then owners, Classic, but with separate entrances for the two screens. The Classic was renamed the Cannon and finally the MGM before closure was announced for 23 February 1995. A last minute bid by a Yorkshire firm, Page Media, brought a welcome reprieve. The second screen, closed for three years following a major fire, was refurbished and the future looked bright – until the appearance of the new multiplex. This 2,000 seater cinema opened to the public in November 1997 and within four months the Tudor fell into receivership. Another profitable Page Media cinema at Malton in North Yorkshire was also forced to close as the company revealed debts of £17,000.

Seventy years earlier the town began to be encircled by new suburban picture houses. By 1919 nine buildings offered moving pictures and queues were quite normal especially at weekends when two separate evening shows were required for the crowds.

Ambitious new schemes came to fruition after the war. In March, the Savoy opened in February 1920, followed a year later by the £25,000 Grand in Manchester Road (Figures 2a & 2b). This later became the second in Huddersfield to be wired for sound. By 1922 the Lyceum brought pictures to the Somerset Road area and finally

Figure 2a. The Palladium style of the Grand Cinema dominated Manchester Road from March 1921 to June 1957. After ownership by Union Cinemas it later became part of the ABC circuit in 1938. Following closure it became a nightclub until demolition in 1995. *Tony Moss collection*

Figure 2b. The interior of the traditional 1920s Grand that seated 852. Were you in the audience for *The Sheik* (1923), *City Lights* (1931) or *The 39 Steps* (1936)? *Tony Moss collection*

in this post-war building boom (Figure 3), Paddock Head's Premier Picture Palace opened with a colour film, *The Romance of Mary Tudor* on Wednesday, 18 October 1922. Huddersfield now boasted twelve cinema screens – half in the centre and the other six in the suburbs.

To keep all these screens filled, the release schedule of movies was bulging. During 1922 seventeen million people went to the pictures each week in the UK - with ninety per cent of the films produced in American studios.

To regulate this boom, a new middleman was emerging in film distribution. Prior to the war, film salesmen provided a print to a cinema for a fixed price. This print was shown and then sold on for screening at smaller cinemas – until the celluloid eventually disintegrated. So by the time the film reached the outer suburbs the scratchy images, the bad jump edits and frequent breakdowns caused much amusement for audiences. The pianist became used to a shower of orange peel and monkey nut shells.

The boom in cinema building and the increasing competition created a need for a major restructuring of the print supply chain. Escalating star demands and increasing production costs forced the film makers to maximise revenue for each movie. Major cinema

Figure 3. Moldgreen's supercinema, the 880 seater Lyceum opened in Wakefield Road in 1922, with the Jackie Coogan film, *Peck's Bad Boy. Tony Moss collection*

exhibition circuits needed to protect their market against smaller operators. To make matters worse, each film had less and less exclusive screen time. Another blockbuster was just a week or two away. The film distributors aim was to capitalise on a films publicity and give it a nationwide release at the most luxurious cinemas where top admission prices could be set.

The distributor took a percentage of the box office and this varied according to the likely public response. A figure of fifty per cent on first release, dropped a few weeks later to maybe thirty-five per cent on second run at the major suburbans. Some three or six months later the smallest and least profitable fleapit would pay twenty-five per cent. Films could often still be showing a year after release.

The power of the distributor increased throughout the twenties as the big films began to be auctioned to the highest bidder. Other booking schemes emerged whereby a package of movies were offered to a chain – these consisted of blockbusters and the less welcome 'lemons'. Even more alarming, these packages were sold blind so that the exhibitor contracted to play the film before any viewing.

Still the cinema boom continued in the town. Next for picturegoers was the Princess in Northumberland Street (Figure 4).

Figure 4. The Princess struggled as an independent cinema for perhaps more years than it should. It also had a chequered early history with many different owners since opening in 1923. A cafe and dance hall was inaugurated in the basement six months after the cinema opened in May. *Tony Moss collection*

Housed in a former woolen exporters warehouse, adjacent to the Tramways office, the Princess was not the first enterprise in the town for Mark Freedman. Back in 1912 he'd converted an old confectionery and toffee works in Viaduct Street into the Olympia Cinema. Three years later he founded the Empire and by 1916 he was promoting the showing of film seasons at the Town Hall.

The new premises for the Princess Cinema cost £8,000 and alterations, including the addition of a café dansant, added another £34,000. The arrival of film star, Peggy Hyland to open the cinema on Whit Sunday 1923 caused traffic gridlock in the vicinity. Perhaps foreseeing the future, Miss Hyland said in her speech, 'It's easy for me to open a picture house, but it's up to you, the audience, the keep it open'. Her latest film, *Shifting Sands*, was then screened for an invited audience. Public performances began two days later on Whit-Monday with D W Griffith's *Way Down East* starring Lillian Gish.

Peggy Hyland's opening words must have echoed in Mark Freedman's ears when the company fell into financial difficulties just four years later. The Leeds Bankrupcy Court heard that except for the first three weeks the company had consistently lost money. Debts within six months of the opening amounted to £24,000. Luckily the Princess was then taken over by manager, Mr. Earnshaw, who took the cinema to great success showing such classics as *Nanook of the North, the Mikado, Hamlet, Pygmalion* and *South Riding.*

The Princess was the last silent cinema to open and the first to be converted to sound. The Picturedrome presented four short sound films in April 1929, then the Empire screened the part sound film, *The Jazz Singer*. Al Jolson's next blockbuster gave the honour to the Princess for the presentation of the first full-length all-talking film in Huddersfield. *The Singing Fool* opened here for an extended and highly successful run from the 13 May 1929. Huddersfield picturegoers packed the Princess for a total of five weeks to see this revolutionary feature.

The coming of *Sonny Boy* changed cinemas forever. During 1930 these picture halls were upgraded to sound, Palace Milnsbridge (26 May), Lockwood (2 June), Savoy Marsh (13 October),Lyceum (17 November), Palladium Birkby (1 December) (Figure 5) and Premier Paddock (15 December). The Tudor House sound cinema was born out of the Hippodrome and opened on 6 December. The Victoria was the only hall to close, but reopened in 1933 as a small theatre. That left the Star in Viaduct Street as the final stronghold of silents

Figure 5. The Palladium in Birkby opened in 1914 and offered escapism during the bleak years of the war. After twenty-three years it was extended and re-named the Carlton in August 1937. *Tony Moss collection*

Figure 6. The frontage of the Regal, Moldgreen, was formerly a private house. This cinema in Wakefield Road was one of a number of Huddersfield cinemas that were opened in the thirties. The Regal premiered its first film in April 1936. In 1952 the proprietors were fined for allowing youngsters under six years of age into a matinee show. *Tony Moss collection*

but even this venue was forced to succumb. Their final silent, *Prince and the Dancer* starring Vivian Gibson was screened on 15 August 1931 and the sound of *Rookery Nook* followed two days later.

Throughout the decade the town continued to be ringed by new cinemas, the Plaza Thornton Lodge (2/3/31), the Waterloo (12/10/31), Regent Fartown (11/11/33), Cosy Nook, Salendine Nook (22/3/34), Regal Moldgreen (6/4/36) (Figure 6), Carlton (old Palladium) Birkby (30/8/27), Lounge Newsome (15/12/37), Rialto Sheepridge (3/11/38), Vale Mirfield (23/10/39) and Majestic (old Star) 25/1/40.

Sunday opening for cinemas was a tortuous fight but was finally allowed from 4 Jan 1948 – by which time we start to sense a sad and prolonged decline of those once mighty entertainment halls.

When the ABC closed in 1983 it was almost symbolic of the end of the golden age of cinema going. This, the former Ritz had brought glamour and showmanship to the town both with films and live shows (Figures 7a & 7b). Many couples would have spent their early

Figure 7a. Built at a cost of £100,000, this really was the town's most impressive supercinema. The Ritz always offered the most up-to-date and glamorous film and stage shows. On the opening night, 10 February 1936, Harold Ramsay rose through the stage to play the organ. Billy Cotton's Broadcasting Band was on stage and high on the big screen was Jessie Matthews in *First a Girl*. *Tony Moss collection*

Figure 7b. The splendid 1930s Ritz auditorium gave perfect sight lines to the 2,036 patrons. Top stars like Alfredo, Elsie and Doris Waters, Wee Georgie Wood, Tessie O'Shea and Norman Evans were big draws in the first few years. After closure in 1982, the building remained boarded up for another three years before demolition. *Tony Moss collection*

courting days in the back row – the choice of film was irrelevant! To be on your own away from the prying eyes of parents and neighbours is often recalled as the most exciting of times.

By the mid 1980s cinema attendances in Britain plummeted to their lowest ever – reaching fifty-three million in 1984. Today audiences have almost tripled since then and the future looks brighter each year – but there's a long way to go to equal the 1946 figure of 1,450 million visits.

The decline in cinema attendances is normally attributed to television, but by 1951 when the BBC programmes began from Holme Moss, the decline was some six years old. Television merely accelerated the process. Massive social changes after the war attacked the movie habit. There was a strong sense of wanting a different way of life. Rationing and 'making do' led to a pent up desire for an end to the old pre-war days. Cinemas to many young people seemed old fashioned – something our parents and grandparents once enjoyed. At the same time the post war baby boom kept many couples at home with little spare cash for town centre leisure.

Another subtle factor was the 1947 balance of payments crisis. At the time the country was coping with a dreadful winter, the Board of Trade decided that too much money was flowing our of Britain, mostly towards America. The President of the Board, Huddersfield's Harold Wilson, decreed that all outgoing credit for America was to be held here in Britain. A major outflow was film receipts and naturally Hollywood reacted swiftly and decisively to this threat to their revenue. Within twenty-four hours the movie moguls stopped any new blockbusters being shown here. Cinemas were quickly forced to bring back older films and the audiences naturally stayed at home. British film studios were encouraged to accelerate their production and under the guidance of J Arthur Rank, Pinewood and Elstree studios began a frantic effort to fill the country's silver screens.

Sadly for Rank and the British film industry, the Government capitulated to Hollywood's threat and did a swift U-turn. Hollywood's finest films flooded back, leaving the British studios floundering. Even when the home grown films were released, British audiences still showed a preference for the stateside musicals, comedies and dramas.

So the decline began as early as 1947 and was never reversed for another four decades. In Huddersfield one by one the cinemas were boarded up. First in the suburbs and then not much later in the town centre. The arrival of BBC Television in 1951 and Granada four years later only served to hasten the decimation. The Grand in Manchester Road closed after thirty-six years, in July 1957. In John William Street the sun set on the Empire in August 1973 after a fifty-eight year history. The power cuts of the early seventies devastated audiences nationwide and by the eighties the rise of video and cable gave exhibition some dismal years. In 1985, the British Film Year, the

ABC chain was receiving eighty per cent of its revenue from just twenty per cent of its cinemas.

The cinema business lives by reinventing itself. It has to repackage the mix to appeal to new generations and in this process the accommodation changes. Some would say this is an improvement from the 1950s cold, unwelcoming fleapits to today's bright sparkling multiplex amphitheatres. Others of course are nostalgic for the huge stalls and balconies that were packed night after night. Whatever your feelings, Huddersfield almost became cinema-less. Thankfully a multiplex came along to allow us to enjoy the enduring magic of big screen movies.

9. NURSES AND NURSING IN HUDDERSFIELD 1870-1960

by Graham Thurgood

OVER THE LAST TWO HUNDRED YEARS Huddersfield has played an important part in the development of nursing and health care. Nurses have worked in a variety of settings and institutions that have through their education schemes provided thousands of trained nurses. General nursing is defined as the care of patients with physical illnesses or injuries and is the intended focus. Littlewood is dealing with psychiatric nursing.[1]

The 'ideology of domesticity' presupposes that women and men are naturally members of distinct spheres of society: women in the 'private' sphere of families and men in the public world of 'work' and business.[2] Nursing may be seen as a way that women gained access to paid work during the nineteenth and twentieth centuries.

During the eighteenth century members of local villages who had special skills or interests in healing did most 'nursing'. Families or friends often cared for the sick in their own homes. With no recognised health care system and medical and surgical treatments either non-existent, primitive or in their infancy, the early nineteenth century social welfare reforms resulted in the Poor Law, that influenced health care, creating the provision of organised institutions. It is not clear what nurses did during the early development of hospitals in Huddersfield as few records exist. It is clear, however, that nurses did care for people and work in an organised way both in institutions and in the community.

The first local hospitals, called Dispensaries, were established in Doncaster (1792), Wakefield (1787) and Halifax (1807).[3] People locally wanted their own so the Huddersfield General Dispensary opened in July 1814 in a rented house in Pack Horse Yard.[4] Known as the Huddersfield and Upper Agbrigg Dispensary, it was for the relief of the industrious poor of the Town and District.[5] About the same time the first workhouse for Huddersfield, was built at Birkby.[6]

The Dispensary functioned more like a First Aid post than a hospital.[7] During the next fourteen years it proved to be 'absolutely inadequate to the demands of a population increasingly engaged in perilous mechanical pursuits, the very instruments of their daily toil a constant menace to life and limb'.[8] By 1828 a Committee had met in the *George Inn* and reported:

> the present building is not adequate to the wants of the sick poor, in this district, it is the unanimous opinion of the meeting that the time is arrived, when an infirmary should be erected, on such a scale, and of such dimensions, as may be co-adequate with the resources and wants of the district.

Evidence of the nurse's role is found in this statement from the same meeting:

> Dispensaries, in many cases, are highly useful; as the professional assistance and attention, which certain patients require, can be supplied at their own dwellings. But in many complaints, this practice is incompatible; as in diseases requiring important surgical operations; cases demanding skill, on the part of professed nurses - and a thousand conveniences not to be found in the destitute habitations of the poor. For such patients, hospitals are indispensable.[9]

This is an early recognition that 'skilled nurses' were required and that nurses were often unskilled and of poor educational and social background.

An Infirmary on New North Road was opened on 29 June 1831 for 'the reception of a limited number of In-patients; more especially for those frequent accidents arising from the extensive use of machinery'.[10] The first Resident Medical Officer was appointed at a salary of £20 a year. The first Matron, a Mrs Newstead, had a similar sum but was to receive a bonus of £5 at the end of the year if she behaved herself.[11] It's not clear what her role was but she was the first of many to hold the title 'Matron' in Huddersfield. Day nurses were paid £8 a year and Night nurses 1s per night.[12] The Matron and Sister ruled the wards, but the nurses tried to make them as comfortable as possible for the patients.[13]

The following (Figure 1) illustrates the work of the nurses in the Infirmary in 1831-32;

Number of patients admitted into the house	137
Number of out-patients	2,920
Average number of patients at one time	20
Patients admitted with broken bones	18
Amputations	12

In 1836

the grand work of the staff did not preclude romance, for one morning the Matron, Miss Clay and the Resident Medical Officer, Mr. Clayton left the infirmary without any fuss and returned an hour later as man and wife, having been married in the interval. But as one of the rules of the Establishment forbade both these functionaries to leave the premises at the same time, the culprits were hauled before a Special Meeting of the Board convened for the purpose and solemnly admonished that their conducts did not again occur.[14]

The Huddersfield Union was formed by an order of the Poor Law Commissioners dated 21 January, 1837. It consisted of thirty-four parishes, and a population of 87,421 made it the second largest in the country.[15] Things were not always good and in 1848 the Huddersfield Workhouse was said to be 'wholly unfitted for a residence for the many scores that are continually crowded into it, unless it be that we desire to engender endemic and fatal disease.'[16] This led to the opening of Deanhouse Workhouse, Holmfirth, in 1862,[17] followed by Crosland Moor Workhouse in 1872.

Twinning noted in 1886 that

One means of creating an interest in Poor Law management would be the publication in each union of an annual report or statement of the workhouse and infirmary with details of expenditure. It will scarcely be believed that only 2 metropolitan Boroughs print and circulate any such statement at present.

This explains the limited records available to confirm what nurses were doing and who they were.[18] She further confirms that the

Workhouse Nursing Association has done good service in this cause during the last 7 years, and has now 60 trained nurses employed in the metropolitan infirmaries and country workhouses. [19]

Twinning also emphasises the importance of the quality of nurses by ensuring the matrons were educated women. She recommended they

received a special training in the care of the sick to fit them for their work, and not, as too often at present, former workhouse officers, with little or no knowledge of sickness.

She also highlights the demise of the pauper nurses by recommending they be excluded from 'all power and authority over the sick.'[20]

With increases in infectious diseases nurses were needed to staff the new isolation hospitals like the one in 1873 at Birkby.[21]

The increasing numbers of nurses is illustrated in 1872-73 when the Huddersfield Infirmary added an additional storey to the main building for nurse's accommodation. The need for nurses at the Infirmary was indicated in 1886 when the average number of beds occupied was eighty-five and total number of patients treated 8,194. With an average length of stay of thirty-four days its clear nurses were needed to care for them.[22]

During the 1890s the Board of Guardians managed nurses in the Workhouse, evidenced by the nurses roles and responsibilities listed below:

- To attend upon the sick in the sick and lying-ill wards, and to administer to them all medicines and medical applications, according to the direction of the Medical Officer.

- To inform the Medical Officer of any defects which may be observed in the arrangements of the sick or lying- in ward.

- To take carp that a light is kept at night in the sick ward.[23]

Nurses are mentioned in relation to the use of 'bed cards' which shows early awareness of the importance of record keeping as

It is desirable that these cards, should, in a great measure, show the history and treatment of each case and they should be carefully preserved.[24]

The Workhouse stressed the nurse's role

is one of very serious responsibility and labour, and requires to be filled by a person of great experience in the treatment of the sick, of great respectability and character, and of diligent and decorous habits. Such person cannot discharge the duties of the office singly, but must have the assistance of others of both sexes; and there is scarcely less need of the same qualities in the persons who are to be assistants than of those required for the chief officer.[25]

This shows a need to employ skilled nurses and is illustrated further by the instructions to nurses –

The Nurse is subject to the direction and control of the Master and Matron, but in the absence of any special direction from them, she will act according to the following instructions: - The sick wards and the female imbecile wards, and all the offices and other premises connected therewith, including the fever wards, will be considered to be under the charge of the Female Nurse and her Assistants.[26]

From the Workhouse records many other aspects of nurses work can be identified including bathing, dressing, care of the dying, eating and drinking, ventilation and that 'no person shall hold the office of Nurse who is not able to read written directions upon medicines.'[27]

In spite of the emergence of hospitals nurses continued to work in patients homes. The national Queen Victoria Jubilee Institution for Nurses (QVJIN) was designed so patients could have visits from trained District Nurses, known as Queens Nurses. It was recognised in June 1897 that the Huddersfield districts where Free nurses had been used were regarded as 'the best friends of the suffering poor.'[28] It was also noted that for the previous twelve years there had been one nurse working in Huddersfield and that she had paid 2,119 free visits.[29] The Huddersfield District Victoria Sick Nurses Association was established in 1897 and at a meeting on 27 July the Association applied to become affiliated with the QVJIN and engage a superintendent and two nurses.[30] It aimed to provide Trained Nurses for the Sick Poor in their homes. The first Superintendent Nurse commenced work on 14 October 1897. Miss Annie Francis Lunn had trained at Macclesfield and St Thomas' for four years, and as a District Nurse trained at the Central Home, Chertsey and Bloomsbury. Her salary was £40 for six months with increases.[31] The first nurse engaged was Nurse Hall, a probationer appointed assistant nurse on 1 November 1897. Her salary was £40 per year and she had a uniform supplied, with ten pence per week housekeeping allowance and 1s for laundry allowance.[32] General conditions for the nurses included having at least one years training in an approved General Hospital or Infirmary, not less than six months approved training in District Nursing and those in County Districts at least three months Midwifery training.

Miss Lunn's Report illustrates the type and quantity of the nurse's work (Figure 2).

Miss Lunn's Report 1897[33]

567 visits from 15 October to 30 November.
3 operations attended.
40 patients entered in register.
3 cases refused.
19 cases on books on 30 November.
37 loans of Invalid appliances, water pillows, clothing.
3 air cushions and thermometer were to be obtained.

In 1898, Clare House, Clare Hill was obtained as a base for three years at £20 per year.[34] Miss Lunn, Head Nurse resigned to go to Northampton and Miss Hall was appointed Superintendent on 19 April 1898 at £40 per year on condition she stayed for two years unless unforeseen circumstances should arrive.[35] Miss Elizabeth Walden was appointed fourth nurse at £30 per year from 12 May 1898. The Corporation arranged for nurses to use tokens instead of pennies on the trams. There is evidence that not all was well with the standard of care provided when Miss Hall, the Superintendent, was 'to investigate complaints about how one of the nurses performed her duties.' Monitoring of the quality of nursing care was important as illustrated by Superintendent inspections of nurses' work. Other District Nursing Associations in Huddersfield had their own geographical boundaries as illustrated on 12 June 1900,

That the Superintendent be instructed that the association do not nurse in the district covered by the Marsh and Lindley Nursing Association without their consent.[36]

The overall high quality and standard of nursing and nurses in the Association was recognised nationally for many years. The Association continued until the 1970s when the local authority took over the provision of district nursing services. Other Associations existed such as the Dalton District Nursing Association.[37] In 1936 there were fourteen other Nursing Associations, not all affiliated to the Queens Institute, working in villages around Huddersfield.[38]

Figures 1 and 2 on pages 112 and 115 provide information about the Huddersfield Associations development and the Queens Nurses work during the 1930-40s.[39]

The Hospital Management Board of Crosland Moor Workhouse laid down rules and regulations for teaching probationer nurses in December 1899 and with three weeks holiday per year set a scale of pay:

1st year = £10
2nd year = £14
3rd year = £18

In 1901 at a Conference of Yorkshire Unions, Huddersfield participated in a scheme to approve the Training and Certification of Workhouse Nursing in Yorkshire. The Yorkshire Poor Law Nursing Board was created consisting of one representative from each Union and the Medical Officer and Lady Superintendent from Unions with

Resident Medical Officers.

The Board set certain rules and guidelines:

1. That Probationer Nurses should be well educated young women of high character.
2. That Probationers be 21 years or over.
3. That Probationers serve a trial period of at least two months, and if found suitable for training enter into an agreement with the Union to train for at least three years.

The Department of Medicine of the Yorkshire College provided theoretical medical and surgical knowledge and tests and issued a Certificate for successful Yorkshire Trained Nurses, known as the Yorkshire Standard Certificate. A Supervising Training Committee, consisting of five Lady Superintendent Nurses set standards and monitored practical efficiency. They provided a Certificate confirming the nurses practical skills. It was hoped 'the certificate of the College will be of great value, and will place Yorkshire Nurses in the foremost rank of their profession.'[40]

By 1902 a scheme of 3-4 year nurse training had been in existence for several years at Crosland Moor Workhouse.

At the Huddersfield Infirmary in 1910 a Wing containing eighteen bedrooms was added to the Home following the addition of another twenty-four bedrooms, indicating the increasing numbers of nurses needed.

During 1900-20 Huddersfield became famous for its work in Infant Welfare developments.[41, 42, 43] Matrons often represented nursing leadership but individual nurses also made considerable contributions by their skilled hard work and loyalty to their patients. One example was Miss Dorothy Wood whose contribution to maternal and child health as a School Nurse in Huddersfield in the 1930-50s continued the earlier pioneering work in public health.[44] Infant Welfare Nurses Miss Mary Tracey and Miss Phoebe England were other local examples.[45] The development of public health, and particularly infant welfare services during the early twentieth century illustrates the important role Huddersfield played in this and in the development of the Health Visiting profession. The growth of eighteenth and nineteenth century local health care has been previously documented.[46, 47]

In 1928 the Child Health and Maternity Care Scheme (MCWS) was described as unique to Huddersfield involving voluntary notification of pregnancy since 1916 and domiciliary visits by lady doctors.[48]

During the 1914-1918 War, Huddersfield Royal Infirmary placed beds at the disposal of the War Office and convoys were admitted direct from the front. A special massage department was equipped with trained staff to deal with the disabled men of the district.[49] The institutions used as War Hospitals included Royds Hall Wood, Paddock used as an Open Air War Hospital and paid for by voluntary subscriptions totalling £30,000. It had between 600 – 2,000 beds. It was open between October 1915 – October 1918 and 17,200 soldiers were accommodated. Also Bradley Gate Sanatorium was used for wounded soldiers and Paddock Council School as an auxiliary hospital.[50] The Denby Dale and Cumberworth, Skelmanthorpe, and Clayton West Military Auxiliary Hospital was operational between October 1916 and February 1919. A letter from the Huddersfield War Hospital on 2 October 1916 identifies that several convalescence homes were used as Military hospitals to relieve pressure on it. They had to meet five criteria, one being to have competent Matrons. The Denby Dale Military Auxiliary Hospital Matron interviews were on 17 November 1916 and Miss Meadows from Cheshire was appointed. On its opening the 'Matron and Miss B Mainprize, Sister, both expressed their satisfaction upon the appearance of the hospital.' Brooches were presented to VAD nurses when the hospital closed on 15 February 1919.[51] In the West Riding there was a shortage of military hospital nurses, and 500 qualified women offered help, with 200 placed in responsible positions demonstrating West Riding women's devotion.[52]

After the First World War the National rate of unemployment for women was higher than in Huddersfield indicating women were able to gain employment more easily in local textile and engineering industries and in healthcare.[53]

In 1921/22 to implement the *Nursing State Registration Act* of 1919, the Hospital Management Board of the Crosland Moor Workhouse appointed a Sister Tutor. In 1929, the Preliminary Training School (PTS) of the Royal Infirmary was established ahead of many prominent hospitals. During PTS, nurses underwent a six-week special course of instruction, consisting of practical, theoretical and invalid cookery work, before entering the wards. This prepared them to enter the hospital with some knowledge of what to expect and greatly helped her and the ward Sister. It meant patients did not have absolutely raw recruits attending them. A full-time Sister Tutor was with the candidates who lived at the school, which was originally at 156 Trinity Street.

During the 1930s the Royal Infirmary continued its general nurse training and was regularly inspected by the General Nursing Council (GNC) who approved training schools. In 1931 Mill Hill Isolation Hospital was approved as a Fever Nurse Training School and a Nurse Training School for TB opened in 1933.[54] Bradley Wood Sanatorium was also inspected by the GNC for providing probationer nurses with training experiences. During this period the local institutions and hospitals had nurse leaders in the form of matrons, examples included Miss McGuthrie Clark at Bradley Wood Sanatorium, Miss E White at Mill Hill Hospital and Miss I Smith at the Municipal Maternity Home, Greenlea Road.[55] Typical of these professionals was Miss E L Long, matron of the Huddersfield Royal Infirmary from July 1928 to November 1958 (Figure 3). She had trained as a registered nurse at Bristol Royal Infirmary. During her thirty years as a matron she founded the Huddersfield Royal Infirmary Old Nurses League and was its chairman and vice-president for many years. She is warmly remembered by many nurses as a strict but kind person who managed the nursing staff very effectively.

During the Second World War Huddersfield continued its war time support as in the First World War. An advert in 1940 requests

Nurses needed at Deanhouse, St Mary's Hospital, near Netherthong. Its was greatly extended for use as a base hospital and it is stated that nurses are urgently needed there. Nursing Auxiliaries are also wanted.[56]

Figure 3. Miss E L Long, matron of the Huddersfield Royal Infirmary from July 1928 to November 1958.

To manage nurses shortages during the war Huddersfield trained over two hundred Auxiliary nurses at the Infirmary between May 1939 to March 1940. Nurse training continued during the war and an advert for Infirmary Probationer Nurses confirms the PTS was a two-month course of lectures and practical work. Probationers should be women of good education aged 18-30. They were paid during the three years training £20, £25, £30 per year with board, uniform and laundry provided free. A resident Sister Tutor coached them.[58]

Post-war developments included the introduction of the National Health Service, changing the structure of health care services but not affecting nurse's work to any great extent.

A unit at Green Lea, Lindley, was available for the admission of private patients and student nurses gained experience there. An Affiliated Training for State Registration existed between the Huddersfield Royal Infirmary and the Women's and Children's St Mary's Hospital, Manchester. The probationers did their Children's training at Booth Hall, Manchester. Some fever-trained nurses did two years general training and gained a combined Hospital Certificate from the Infirmary. On 27 September 1946 the GNC Education and Examination Committee approved the withdrawal of the scheme of affiliation between Mirfield Memorial Hospital and Huddersfield Royal Infirmary and Mirfield Memorial Hospital was removed from the list of approved Training Schools. On 19 July 1947 the provisional approval for a Training School for Male Nurses, for two years, was approved by the GNC for the Huddersfield Royal Infirmary.[60]

The Queen Victoria Jubilee Nursing Institute Inspectors continued to visit the Huddersfield Victoria District Nurses Association. During the 1940-50s nurses gradually started using cars. Petrol was two shillings (20p) a gallon and the cars were kept in garages behind the nurses' home. A Mr Pearce worked in the boiler house in the basement and looked after the cars and taught the nurses to drive. Morris Minor and Ford Prefect cars were bought later. The home housed about twenty nurses, two Matrons, a housekeeper and a maid called Mary. Nurses were called 'Miss' not Nurse and they were on duty 9am - 1pm, 3pm - 6pm and 7pm - 10pm. Queen's Nurses wore Queens Institute of District Nursing Badge on their hats, and the Bronze Medal with nurses number engraved on the back of it, was worn around the neck on white and blue silk cord.[61] (A goup of nurses of the period is shown in Figure 4)

By 1947 Mill Hill Hospital had twenty nurses (Figures 5 & 6), the

Figure 4. Queens District nurses in 1947.

Figure 5. Nurse Anna Foster with two patients on a lawn behind Ward 5 or 6 of Mill Hill Hospital, Dalton, looking towards Waterloo, between 1951 and 1953.

Figure 6. Staff Nurse Anna Foster with student nurse Barbara Lukash (nee Gerard) on the lawn behind the wards in 1953 with patients nearly ready to go home. The end of Ward 6 Mill Hill Hospital is in the background.

Nurses Home had twenty-eight single rooms and they worked ninety-six hours per fortnight. Matron Miss E White coached the nurses and they went to the Technical College for anatomy and physiology and hygiene lectures. One of the most unpleasant of the nurse's tasks must have been the disposal of sputum by cleaning, disinfecting, and boiling the mugs.[62]

Following the war a second level of nurses emerged called assistant or pupil nurses, eventually known as State Enrolled Nurses (SEN). As the Royal Infirmary continued to provide training for State Registered Nurses (SRN), the other local hospitals provided assistant nurse training. In 1947 a proposed Training Scheme for Pupil Nurses with St Luke's Hospital and Holme Valley Memorial Hospital was submitted to the General Nursing Council.[63] Mill Hill Hospital and Bradley Wood Sanatorium were also included.

By 1951 the fever nursing students at Mill Hill joined their Huddersfield Royal Infirmary general nursing colleagues for the PTS which had moved to Ellerslie, Blacker Road.[64] By 1957 Matron, Miss E White had retired from Mill Hill and a Miss E Howarth was appointed on 1 September 1957. Following changes in the incidence of infectious disease by 1957 there was no longer any Fever Training at Mill Hill due to lack of experiences and TB wards. It was reported that a thirty-four-bed unit for chronic sick men was to open at the end of 1957.[65]

Nurses continued to work in a variety of settings during the 1950s (Figures 7 & 8). At the Huddersfield Royal Infirmary and other local hospitals nurses continued to be trained. Trained nurses worked in both

Figure 7. Staff Nurse Janet Velma, Huddersfield Royal Infirmary, 1956. This illustrated local staff nurse's pale lilac striped dress including cap and apron after just qualifying from a four year training period.

Figure 8. Huddersfield Royal Infirmary. Annual Re-union dinner of the HRI Nurses' League at Ellerslie, then the Nurse Training School in 1959. The picture shows the Reverend Poole, Church of England Chaplain and Mrs Horsfall, the President of the League.

hospital and community based areas. Due to changing demands in health care-nurses were to have the opportunity to work in the new Huddersfield Royal Infirmary when it opened in the 1960s.

Acknowledgements

The author would like to thank the following people for their help and advice: My PhD research supervisors - Professor Peter Bradshaw, Professor David Taylor and Dr Brian Roberts. The Wellcome Trust for their financial support by providing a research expenses grant. Mrs E A Hilary Haigh, Huddersfield University Archivist. Staff of the West Yorkshire Archive Service, Wakefield. Staff of the West Yorkshire Archive Service, Kirklees. Staff of the Public Record office, Kew Gardens, London. Stephen Carter, Manager, *Huddersfield Daily Examiner* Archive Library. All the retired nurses who have provided information in the course of the author's research.

Photographs: Thanks for permission to use the photographs are due to the *Huddersfield Daily Examiner* Archive Library and Kirklees Photographic Archive, Community History Service.

The following retired nurses, Mrs Marion Dyson, Mrs Eileen Galvin, Miss Margaret Kirkbride, Mrs Barbara Lukash, Mrs Janet Velma, Mrs Florence Wimpenny.

Notes and References

1. Littlewood, A, *A History of Storthes Hall.* Work in progress, due for publication summer 2002.
2. Women in Society. Ideology of Domesticity. 27th March 2002.
http://www.sociologyonline.co.uk/WomenGender.htm#Col12
http://www.sociologyonline.co.uk/WomenGender.htm#Col12
3. Marland, H, 1992 'Health Care in nineteenth-century Huddersfield' in Haigh, H (Ed) *Huddersfield a Most Handsome Town*. Kirklees Cultural Services. 597-630.
4. *Ibid.*
5. *Huddersfield Royal Infirmary, an Epitome* nd. (*c*1921) gives a brief history with illustrations of exterior and some interiors. J Allan Hanson and Son Ltd. Oldham. B 362.11. Kirklees Local Library.
6. *Official Handbook of Her Majesty's Diamond Jubilee Celebration*. County Borough of Huddersfield Walker, J L Alderman/Major. 22nd June 1897, The Advertiser Press, Ltd Huddersfield. B 900 Kirklees Local History Library.
7. Grainger, J, *Healing in Huddersfield*. p23. Huddersfield (training home) 1897-1947. Queen's Institute of District Nursing: Records. PRO 30/63/495.
8. *Official Handbook of Her Majesty's Diamond Jubilee Celebration*. County Borough of Huddersfield Walker, J L Alderman/Major. 22 June 1897 The Advertiser Press Ltd., Huddersfield. B 900 Kirklees Local History Library.
9. KC 311 18/12 Huddersfield and Upper Agbrigg Infirmary. Kirklees, West Yorkshire Archive Service.
10. Schofield, I, 1996 The Heritage of Huddersfield. Chpt. Poorhouse to the National Health Service. P. 144-8. *The Huddersfield Daily Examiner* and Kirklees Cultural Services. Derby, Breedon Books Publishing Company Limited.
11. KC 311 18/12 Huddersfield and Upper Agbrigg Infirmary. Kirklees, West Yorkshire Archive Service.
12. *Ibid.*
13. Schofield, I, 1996 *The Heritage of Huddersfield*. Chpt. Poorhouse to the National Health Service, p144-8. *The Huddersfield Daily Examiner* and Kirklees Cultural Services. Derby, Breedon Books Publishing Company Limited.
14. *Huddersfield Royal Infirmary, an Epitome* nd. (c1921) gives a brief history with illustrations of exterior and some interiors. p35. J Allan Hanson and Son Ltd. Oldham. B 362.11. Kirklees Local Library.
15. Knott, J, 1986 *Popular Opposition to the 1834 Poor Law*. London, Croom Helm.
16. *Leeds Mercury*, 5 Feb, 1848.
17. Marland, H, 1992 'Health Care in nineteenth-century Huddersfield' in Haigh, H (Ed) *Huddersfield a Most Handsome Town*. Kirklees Cultural Services. 597-630.

18. Twinning, L, 1886, *Workhouse Cruelties. Nineteenth Century,* November, p. 709.

19. *Ibid.* p710.

20. *Ibid.*

21. Marland, H, 1992 'Health Care in nineteenth-century Huddersfield' in Haigh, H (Ed) *Huddersfield a Most Handsome Town.* Kirklees Cultural Services pp. 597-630.

22. Johnson, H J. *Your Hospital.* p10. Huddersfield (training home) 1897-1947. Queen's Institute of District Nursing: Records. PRO 30/63/495.

23. Hall, J 1895 *Huddersfield Union Guardians' Handbook. Handbook for the Use and Guidance of the Guardians.* J Hall Clerk of the Guardians. Enlarged edition from 1885 version incorporating changes since the *Local Government Act* of 1894.

24. *Ibid*

25. *Ibid*

26. *Ibid*

27. *Ibid*

28. *Official Handbook of Her Majesty's Diamond Jubilee Celebration.* County Borough of Huddersfield. Walker, JL Alderman/Major. 22 June 1897, The Advertiser Press Ltd Huddersfield. B900, Local History Library, Kirklees.

29. *Ibid.*

30. KC 291 Huddersfield and District Victoria Sick Poor Nurses Association Minute Book. Kirklees, West Yorkshire Archive Service.

31. Queen Victoria's Jubilee Institute for Nurses. Inspectors Report 18th October 1897. PRO 30/63/495.

32. *Ibid.*

33. KC 291 Huddersfield and District Victoria Sick Poor Nurses Association Minute Book. Kirklees, West Yorkshire Archive Service.

34. *Ibid.*

35. Queen Victoria's Jubilee Institute for Nurses. Inspectors Report 13/14 April 1898. PRO 30/63/495.

36. KC 291 Huddersfield and District Victoria Sick Poor Nurses Association Minute Book. Kirklees, West Yorkshire Archive Service.

37. *Nursing Illustrated* 14 June 1940. p467. Archives and Special Collections, Learning Centre, University of Huddersfield.

38. Irving, M, *District Nursing.* p27. Huddersfield (training home) 1897-1947. Queen's Institute of District Nursing: Records. PRO 30/63/495.

39. Queen Victoria Jubilee Institute for Nurses. PRO 30/63/495.

40. Training and Certification of Workhouse Nursing in Yorkshire. Scheme approved at Conference of Yorkshire Unions held at Leeds, 29th June 1901. Report of Committee appointed by the Conference of Yorkshire Unions, held at the Union Offices, Leeds, on the 8th January, 1901, Approval of Scheme. P/ HU/ zz/ 33, Kirklees, West Yorkshire Archive Service.

41. Parton, C, 1981 *Liberal Individualism and Infant Mortality: The Infant Welfare Movement in Huddersfield 1900-18.* MA Thesis, Huddersfield University.

42. Parton, C, 1983 'Infant welfare movement in early 20th Century Huddersfield' *Journal of Regional and Local Studies,* 3, 2, Winter. Huddersfield Local Library. B 362.7.

43. Marland, H 1993 *A pioneer in infant welfare: the Huddersfield Scheme 1903–1920.* Society for the Social History of Medicine, 25-50.

44. Thurgood, G, 2001 *Dorothy Wood. In Huddersfield.* Ottakars Local History Series. Compiled by Taylor, N P pp. 27-33. Stroud, Tempus Publishing Limited.

45. Report of the medical Officer of Health (Dec 1944) for the years 1939 – 43. Wakefield Archives C381/ 1/47 County Borough of Huddersfield. Wakefield, West Yorkshire Archive Service.

46. Marland, H, 1991, 'Lay and Medical Conceptions of Medical Charity during the Nineteenth Century. The Case of the Huddersfield General Dispensary and Infirmary'. In Barry, J and Jones, C, *Medicine and Charity before the Welfare State.*

47. Marland, H, 1992, 'Health Care in Nineteenth Century Huddersfield' in Haigh, EAH (Ed.) 1992 *Huddersfield, A Most Handsome Town.* Chpt 23, pp. 597 – 630. Huddersfield, Kirklees Cultural Services.

48. KX 391 Keeling M J, 1998 'Public Health and Housing in the County Borough of Huddersfield 1928-38'. BA (Hons) 20/02/1998. Kirklees, West Yorkshire Archive Service.

49. *Huddersfield Royal Infirmary, an Epitome* nd. (c1921) gives a brief history with illustrations of exterior and some interiors. J Allan Hanson and Son Ltd. Oldham. B 362.11. Kirklees Local Library.

50. Balmforth, O, *1918 Jubilee History of the Corporation of Huddersfield 1868–1918.* Huddersfield, Corporation of Huddersfield, p86.

51. KC 799 14/8 Military Auxiliary Hospital Denby Dale. May 1919 *Official Souvenir. History of*

the Denby Dale and Cumberworth, Skelmanthorpe, and Clayton West Military Auxiliary Hospital. Dec 1916-Feb 1919.

52. *Ibid.*

53. Phillips, C, 1995 *The Impact of the First World War upon the Status and Employment of Women with reference to Huddersfield*, p68. MA Thesis. University of Huddersfield.

54. GNC, Education and Examination Committee, 7th December 1938. DT 35 42, PRO.

55. *Huddersfield Royal Infirmary Old Nurses League Newsletter*, Christmas 1958.

56. KX 391 Keeling MJ 1998 *Public Health and Housing in the County Borough of Huddersfield 1928-38.* BA (Hons) 20/02/1998. Kirklees, West Yorkshire Archive Service.

57. *The Huddersfield County Borough Directory 1937* Huddersfield, Alfred Jubb and Sons Ltd. Local History Library, Kirklees.

58. *Nursing Illustrated*, 10 May, 1940. p335. Archives and Special Collections, Learning Centre, University of Huddersfield.

59. *Nursing Illustrated*, 1 March, 1940, p749. Archives and Special Collections, Learning Centre, University of Huddersfield.

60. *Nursing Illustrated*, 1 March–30 August 1940. P. xi. Archives and Special Collections, Learning Centre, University of Huddersfield.

61. Huddersfield Royal Infirmary. 1946. GNC Records. DT 35/42. PRO

62. Huddersfield Royal Infirmary. 1947. GNC Records. DT 35/42. PRO.

63. Information provided by retired nurses during interviews.

64. GNC Report. 1947. DT 33/ 265. PRO.

65. *Ibid.*

66. GNC Report. 1951. DT 33/ 265. PRO.

67. GNC Report. 1957. DT 33/ 265. PRO.

10. An Artists' Colony in Leeds Road

by Richard Stakes

Introduction

J B PRIESTLEY IN HIS NOVEL 'THE GOOD COMPANIONS' (1928) described football as 'hurtling with conflict and yet passionate and beautiful in its arts'. There has been a colony of artists practising their trade up Leeds Road in Huddersfield since the early part of the twentieth century. This group may not be known for its painting, sculpture or its literary skills. Yet during this time they have contributed to the area's dramatic productions. As with the musical tradition in the area, Huddersfield Town Association Football Club is known across the world. In their history the club has scaled the footballing heights as well as plummeting its depths. Few clubs have had such contrasting fortunes through their history. However, at the beginning of the twenty-first century, the success of 'The Terriers', as they are affectionately known, is such a long time ago it is but a faint memory for even its oldest supporters. Nevertheless, when discussing local artistic and cultural influences some of the major contributions to the history of the blue and whites should be celebrated here.

Origins

Huddersfield's winter sporting tradition lies in rugby, particularly rugby league. Indeed, the professional rugby code was initiated at the *George Hotel* in the town in 1894, as was the Super-League some hundred years later. At the turn of the twentieth century Huddersfield was regarded in sporting circles as a rugby league town, with a successful professional club based in the Fartown area.

Nevertheless, the decision to form a professional association football club was taken in 1908. Initially, until 1910 the club played in the Midland League at Leeds Road. The ground was a poor affair. The *Answers Book of Football* (1935) provides a story that the grandstand at Leeds Road was so ramshackle that during the 1908-09 season spectators were asked not to stamp their feet! Nevertheless, (Figure 1) Town gained election to the Football League Second Division for the start of the 1910-1911 season. In the years up to the

Figure 1. A general view of Leeds Road taken in the early 1980s. *Courtesy of Huddersfield Examiner*

cessation of league football in 1915 Town's progress was largely uneventful. The club made little impact on the field before the cessation of League football in 1915. Their off-field financial problems were much greater, to the extent that in early November 1919 the directors announced the club was £25,000 in debt. At the time this was a massive amount of money and there was some doubt as to the future continuance of the club.

As an answer to the problems the club announced they were to leave Leeds Road for Elland Road, Leeds, the home of the now defunct Leeds City club. Leeds City had been forced to disband as a result of a FA investigation of their finances. The directors felt the opportunity for success in Leeds was much better, with a greater potential to draw in bigger crowds. The people of Huddersfield were horrified at the suggestion. This resulted in a massive propaganda campaign, as well as popular demonstrations to keep the club in the town. Despite rumours that the ground had been sold to a local manufacturing company, sufficient funds was quickly raised and after some months of hard bargaining the continuance of football at Leeds Road was secured.

The glory years
It is arguable that a football club has never turned the corner more

dramatically both on and off the pitch than Huddersfield Town. For the rest of the 1919-1920 season attendance at home matches rose massively. Where at the beginning of the season gates were around three thousand by the end of it the average was twenty thousand. Even more remarkably the players also rose to the occasion, finishing the season by winning promotion to the first division. During the season they lost only six of forty-two league games, conceding thirty-eight goals.

This success was not a 'flash in the pan', a one-season wonder. Rather, for the rest of the inter-war period, Huddersfield Town could claim to be among the best in the land. Without doubt for much of the nineteen-twenties they were undisputedly the best in land. In the period between 1920 and 1929 the 'Terriers' were league champions three times in consecutive seasons (1923-26) and runners-up twice (1926-27 and 1927-28). During this period they were also FA Cup finalists three times (1920, 1922 and 1928) winning the trophy once in 1922. The club also won the FA Charity Shield in 1922.

The three consecutive league championships were, at the time, unique in English football. Huddersfield Town, along with Arsenal in the 1930s and Manchester United in the 1990s are the only clubs to have managed this feat. Although still good times the 1930s were by no means as successful for Town. In the league championship some excellent seasons were noted, particularly in the early part of the decade. A best position of runners-up was achieved in 1933-34 and third place was recorded in 1935-36. However, the immediate pre-war years were much more of a struggle for the club. Key players left or grew older and were not replaced as successfully. This lead to a greater level of inconsistency of results than had been the case for the previous fifteen years. Nevertheless, during this time Town held on to their first-division status without too many real difficulties.

It is worth noting that Town, despite any real success in the league programme, continued to have more successful campaigns in the FA Cup. They reached two further Wembley finals (in 1930 and 1938). However, success at the final hurdle eluded them as they lost on both occasions.

The success of the club in the inter-war years was based on the success of some of its most influential players, many of whom were regarded as artists of the contemporary game. These master craftsmen included, among others, Alex Jackson who was described as having film star looks and often regarded by football reporters as both talented and irrepressible. Alex is perhaps best remembered as one of the 1928 'Wembley Wizards', in the Scotland team that beat

England 5-1. Other artistic talents included Roy Goodall, a player of great repute described in the 1934 *Littlewood's Football Annual* as a player who 'kicks cleanly, tackles cleanly and plays cleanly' (p. 21) and Sam Wadsworth, described by Bryon Butler (1988) as 'the cornerstone of the defensive line-up in the championship winning seasons.'

International players

Huddersfield Town's success is reflected in the number of players who have been called up by their country for full international honours. It is perhaps not surprising that most of these players were representing their country during the inter-war years, at a time when Town were at their most successful. Although the majority of international players on Town's books have represented England, their first full international was J J McAuley, who represented Northern Ireland in six internationals between 1911 and 1913.

The first Huddersfield Town player to represent England in a full international was J G Cock (v. Northern Ireland, in 1920). F E Bullock (who also played against Northern Ireland in 1921) followed him. Roy Goodall, usually a right back, represented England twenty-five times between 1926 and 1934. Other players from the same era who played for England included G Brown (nine times 1927-33) E. H. Taylor (eight times from 1923-26) Sam Wadsworth (eight caps 1922-27) and W H Smith (three caps in two years, 1922 and 1928). H Turner played twice for England in 1932. Clem. Stephenson, who was later a long-term manager of the Town, played once for England (v. Wales in 1924). T Wilson also played one full international, against Scotland (in 1928 debacle at Wembley).

In the period before the outbreak of war in September 1939, C K Willingham was Huddersfield's most consistent player in the England side, representing his country twelve times from 1937-1939. A Young played for his country nine times between 1937 and the outbreak of world war two, while A Beasley gained a sole international place, against Scotland in 1939.

Scotland called on Alex Jackson's services fourteen times between 1926 and 1930. It was as a Huddersfield player that he won most of his seventeen international caps. D M Steele played in all the home internationals for Scotland in 1923. Huddersfield Town players again represented Northern Ireland during the inter-war period. L Cumming played in two internationals for his country in 1929, while W E Hayes played for them four times in 1938 and 1939, once with H Baird (v. England, 1939). The sole representative in the full Welsh side between 1919 and 1939 was D G Evans (v. Scotland 1929).

Although in the post-war period Town has had fewer players gaining international honours the list that did so contains some outstanding stars of the game. Undoubtedly the most famous is Ray Wilson, a local boy who played as a full back for Town throughout his career, was called up by England sixty three times between 1960 and 1968. Those appearances included a full set of caps in the successful 1966 World Cup campaign. Others who represented England included Bob Stainforth (eight caps in 1954 and 1955) Harold Hassall (five caps between 1951 and 1954), Bill McGarry (four caps between 1954 and 1956),Vic. Metcalfe, who played for England twice in 1951, and Mike O'Grady who played one international as a Town player in 1963.

Welsh representation in the post-war was limited to two players being called up for full international caps. 'Joey' Jones gained the final half-dozen of his seventy-two caps as a Town player in 1986. Dick Krzywicki also gained two caps for Wales in 1970 while at Leeds Road. Northern Ireland also selected two Huddersfield players in their international sides. McKenna played seven times between 1950 and 1952, while C Galloghy played twice in the 1951 end of season 'home' international series.

The Republic also culled three players from Leeds Road. Michael Meagan played a total of twelve times for his country from 1965-68, Pat Sayward gained four of his caps between 1961 and 1963 and W E Hayes gained two caps for the greens in the 1947 season. Scotland's representation was small but significant. Denis Law, like his illustrious predecessor, Alex Jackson arrived in Huddersfield from Aberdeen (Figure 2). He, however, found fame and fortune

Figure 2. Denis Law in white shirt scores the first goal in Town's 3-1 victory against Peterborough United on 26 January 1957. The crowd at Leeds Road that day was 48,735. *Courtesy of the Huddersfield Examiner*

playing for both Manchester clubs as well as in Italy, but not before he had gained the first six of his fifty-five full international caps as a Huddersfield Town player (1959 and 1960).

Herbert Chapman

Perhaps the greatest artist of them all at Leeds Road, and certainly one who should be remembered some seventy years afterwards, is the manager of two of the three championship winning teams – Herbert Chapman. Herbert, a red-faced, bullish Yorkshireman, arrived at Leeds Road in 1922 and left for Arsenal in 1925. Although a moderate player in his own right, perhaps best remembered for his yellow boots, Chapman became a manger whose thinking was ahead of all his contemporaries. His first managerial position, at the above-mentioned defunct Leeds City, had been abruptly terminated in 1919. His days at Huddersfield and Arsenal provided him with the opportunity to show his managerial skills.

Chapman was a good talker who was a flamboyant, yet shrewd and tough businessman. Some of the tales of his transfer dealings with chairmen of other clubs boarded on the apocryphal. He was a punctilious disciplinarian at the same time as being an excellent motivator, who kept a keen concern for the welfare of all his players. He had a natural ability to recognise and develop talent, taking many of his best signings from lower-division clubs. His Arsenal side also won the championship in 1931 before completing, in Huddersfield style, three successive championships (1932-35). By the time of his premature death in January 1934 his influence stretched beyond the world of football. Perhaps his longest standing influence and the best comment to his powers of persuasion, as well as a testament to his memory, remains the change of name made to the local underground station for the Highbury ground. Chapman persuaded London Transport, with all its concomitent costs, to change the name from Gillespie Road to Arsenal.

Post war years

The inter-war period was a hard act to follow and not surprisingly the post war period has not been so successful for 'The Terriers'. After six years of virtually constant struggle Town were relegated for the first time from the first division at the close of the 1951-52 season. Although top division status was regained after only one season, with a defence that remained unchanged throughout the forty-two-match programme, the blue and whites were relegated again in 1956. Despite the influence of Bill Shankley for four seasons from 1956,

Figure 3. The last game played at Leeds Road, 30 April 1994.

fourteen seasons of second division football passed before the club experienced a brief elevation to the first division again (1970-72). However, most alarming of all was the subsequent slide down the divisions, culminating in five seasons in the basement division of the Football League (1975-80). Cup competitions provided no real success either. The best the club managed was as semi-finalists in the League Cup competition in the 1967-68 season. How the mighty were fallen! (Figure 3)

With the slide in the club's fortunes, attendance plummeted and Leeds Road fell into some disrepair. The need for change was made the more imperative in the aftermath of the Bradford City fire in 1985, and the subsequent *Taylor Report* on crowd safety at sports grounds. By that time the ground that had once hosted international fixtures and received crowds of over sixty-seven thousand had regular attendances only one tenth of that. The ground was also in need of revamping and repair. The barrel roof at the popular end was in need of repair. The vast covered terrace opposite the main stand was severely under-used, while the electronic scoreboard at the open end of the ground (the first in the country) had been vandalised and left in a state of disrepair. What the club needed now was someone to make a dramatic impact equivalent to that in November 1919.

Figure 4. The McAlpine Stadium just before kick-off.

The recommendations of the *Taylor Report*, produced as a consequence of the fifty-six deaths at Valley Parade, Bradford, was to galvanise activity in Huddersfield to such an extent that the club left Leeds Road for a new ground, built in the open space behind it. The last match at the old ground was played on 30 April 1994, with the necessary move taking place during the close season. This new ground, called the McAlpine Stadium after its sponsor and builder, was not merely dramatic, rather it was revolutionary (Figure 4). The semicircular design of all four stands provided a vastly different setting from its gloomy predecessor across the way. This change of venue also acted as a spur to Town's fortunes on the field and, in a far more positive atmosphere around the club; second division status was regained briefly in the 1990s.

In the immediate post-war period Town had its share of international players. These included Harold Hassell, Bill McGarry (later manager of Wolves) and Vic. Metcalfe all of whom represented England, as well as the mercurial Irishman, Peter Docherty. Willie Watson was one of the last double internationals who also represented Yorkshire and England at cricket.

However, from the mid-1950s onwards Town have largely become a feeder club for others to benefit from, and have kept going as a result of the nurture and later transfer of talented players to other clubs. Some of these youngsters have gone onto international fame and acclaim. Most spectacularly, these have included Denis Law (Manchester United and Scotland) Trevor Cherry (Leeds United and England), and Frank Worthington (Leicester City and England).

Modern heroes

Denis Law was a Scot who came to Huddersfield as a teenager in the 1950s and played for Town from 1956 to the turn of the decade. After he left Leeds Road initially he went to Manchester City then Torino in Italy, before finding over ten years of fame at Old Trafford. With United Denis Law teamed up with an Irishman (George Best) and an Englishman (Bobby Charlton). However despite the obvious tag, this trio was no joke. Far from it! Law, Charlton and Best became one of the most effective attacking forces, both in the first division, and latterly, in Europe. At United Law won virtually every honour available at club level. These included the League Championship (1965, 1967) the FA Cup (1963) and the European Cup in 1968. He was voted European Footballer of the Year in 1964 and played a total of fifty-five times for Scotland.

Because of his youthfulness, Law's influence at Leeds Road was less than elsewhere where he played; nevertheless, he remains at fifteen years and ten months 'The Terriers' youngest debutant. In his sixty-eight appearances for the club he scored sixteen goals. However, like Frank Worthington a decade later, he was, in the late nineteen-fifties, among the best-known names to both commentators and fans throughout the land as a 'hot property'. His youthful talent and immense potential was first recognised while wearing the blue and white stripes.

Frank Worthington was a Huddersfield Town player for over eight years, from 1964-72 (Figure 5). In this period Frank made nearly two hundred first team appearances and scored over fifty goals. He joined The Terriers as a schoolboy and left as an established first division player. During this period of time he had also represented his country twice at under twenty-one level, scoring one goal. Subsequent to his departure from Leeds Road he represented his country in full internationals eight times. As well as his time at Leicester he also played in the top division in England for five other clubs, including, Bolton Wanderers, Birmingham City, Leeds United, Sunderland and Southampton. Latterly, displaying his commitment to the playing side of the game, he turned out for a number of lower division clubs making his last appearance for fourth division Stockport County on 22 April 1988.

Although Frank was a well-travelled professional footballer his

Figure 5. From left to right: Ray Wilson, Vic Metcalfe, Denis Law, Trevor Cherry and Frank Worthington gather to commemorate the laying of the centre-spot plaque at the former Leeds Road ground in 1999. *Courtesy of the Huddersfield Examiner*

association with the West Riding of Yorkshire and Huddersfield in particular is strong. He is, relatively at least, a local lad, born in Shelf, a small village on the Halifax/Bradford road, in November 1948. Frank was one of the most flamboyant players in the age of flamboyance in the 1970s. He has been variously described as a genius, a flair player with a cavalier attitude and, more appropriately, one of the most gifted players of his generation. Perhaps more significantly from the spectators point of view, Frank was described by Bill Maynard, in a most readable autobiography, *One Hump or Two, the Frank Worthington Story* (1994) as a player who was worth the price of entry to the game merely to see him go through his warm-up routine. An accolade indeed, with more than a grain of truth in it. Frank was an entertainer wherever he went – one of a long line of beguiling artists who have provided both passion and beauty in Leeds Road for nearly a hundred years.

11. QUARMBY FOLD FOLK

by Vivien Teasdale

A 'FOLD' CAN MEAN either 'doubled or bent back on itself' or 'an enclosure for domestic animals'. Quarmby Fold probably means the former since it is built on the hillside, winding back from the junction of Oakes Road South and Haughs Road. Starting in medieval times as a settlement growing up around Quarmby Hall, it presaged the later yards of Huddersfield, by building the homes facing inwards around a central court. Cottages, soundly built in the 1840s, were in need of repair a century later (Figure 1). It is possible the area would have been cleared but a conservation order ensured that its unspoiled buildings were preserved to show us the type of houses unique to Huddersfield.

Figure 1. Ordnance Survey Map, 1907. Scale – 25″ to 1 mile.

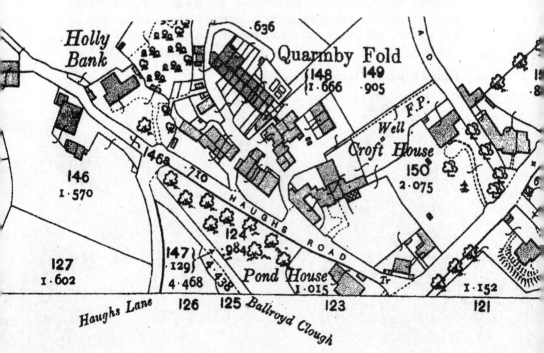

But houses are just bricks, or in this case mostly Yorkshire stone, and mortar. It is the people who make an area what it is. Looking back from the beginning of the twenty-first century to the beginning of the twentieth century, who would we have met and what would they have been doing?

Employers

Not surprisingly the vast majority would have been involved in the woollen industry and many in the area became part of the growing upper middle classes. Some started in the early years with a smallholding and workshop before developing into employers themselves. Thomas Stork, whose father Joseph had begun a yarn spinning mill together with a small sheep farm, lived in Burnhill House which fronts onto Haughs (pronounced Horgs) Road. The family had lived in and around Huddersfield for over thirty years (Figure 2).

Arthur Priestley had started out as a designer of worsted cloth, moving from Lindley into the Fold to accommodate his growing family. By 1901 he was a manufacturer on his own account, employing others to make and design the cloth. Many of his family followed him into various branches of the trade – one daughter, Eliza, became a saleswoman in a draper's shop, Lilian was a dressmaker, and Susan was a bookkeeper. His son, Arthur Fielding Priestley, became manager of a large local mill – Park Valley Mills in

Figure 2. Burnhill House, Haughs Road.

Figure 3. Holly Bank House.

Lockwood owned by Messrs Thornton, Marsden & Co. A F Priestley became a prominent member of the local community, helped by being a Freemason. He was Treasurer of the Huddersfield Textile Society, Director of the Longwood Penny Bank and member of Oakes Baptist Church. His funeral in 1948 was attended by many local dignitaries.

Over thirty years previously Thomas Hall had lived in the Fold, purchasing and farming land around the area, though his son George chose to become a draper's apprentice. After Thomas' death the family moved away into New Hey Road, partially supported by George's earnings when he became an assistant in the draper's shop, whilst his younger sister, Clara, earned a living as a governess. But George had ambitions and was prepared to work for them. By the 1890s he had moved back to Quarmby Fold, but not to the little cottages. His business in King Street was expanding, supplying high quality goods and George was able to afford to purchase Holly Bank, a large stone built house, set in its own grounds just outside Quarmby Fold.

George continued to prosper. He became one of the first in the area to own a car – by 1920 he was the proud owner of a Renault 2 seater in 'puttee' colour (khaki) – and he had many investments in stocks and shares as well as extensive land holdings around Huddersfield (Figure 3).

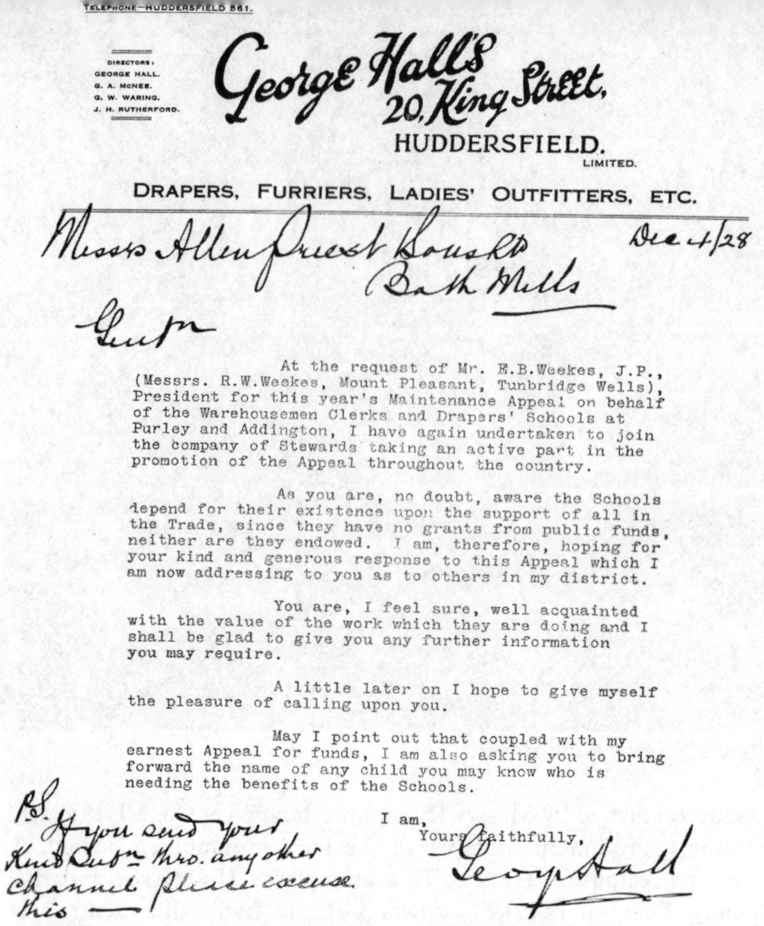

TELEPHONE—HUDDERSFIELD 561.

DIRECTORS:
GEORGE HALL.
G. A. McNEE.
G. W. WARING.
J. H. RUTHERFORD.

George Hall's
20, King Street,
HUDDERSFIELD.
LIMITED.

DRAPERS, FURRIERS, LADIES' OUTFITTERS, ETC.

Messrs Allen Priest Hough Ld Dec 4/28
Bath Mills

Gentⁿ

At the request of Mr. E.B.Weekes, J.P., (Messrs. R.W.Weekes, Mount Pleasant, Tunbridge Wells), President for this year's Maintenance Appeal on behalf of the Warehousemen Clerks and Drapers' Schools at Purley and Addington, I have again undertaken to join the Company of Stewards taking an active part in the promotion of the Appeal throughout the country.

As you are, no doubt, aware the Schools depend for their existence upon the support of all in the Trade, since they have no grants from public funds, neither are they endowed. I am, therefore, hoping for your kind and generous response to this Appeal which I am now addressing to you as to others in my district.

You are, I feel sure, well acquainted with the value of the work which they are doing and I shall be glad to give you any further information you may require.

A little later on I hope to give myself the pleasure of calling upon you.

May I point out that coupled with my earnest Appeal for funds, I am also asking you to bring forward the name of any child you may know who is needing the benefits of the Schools.

I am,
Yours faithfully,
Geo Hall

P.S. If you send your Kind Subⁿ thro. any other channel please excuse this —

Figure 4. Letter from George Hall to associates.

Not everything in life had been easy for the family. Though George had two surviving daughters – Margaret and Elaine – another daughter Dorothy, born in 1888, had died aged just 6½ months old. Perhaps it was this which made him a supporter of the Warehousemen, Clerks and Drapers' Schools charity which had two schools in the London area for needy children. Money was raised by 'Stewards' who used their business and social standing to persuade others to donate. George wrote to many businesses in the area, and many responded with the required guineas (Figure 4).

The family probably would have known the Haighs who lived in Pond House, which stood at the corner of Haugh's Road and Quarmby Fold. Sam was a cloth dealer and woollen merchant buying the pieces from small manufacturers and selling them on. At the early age of twenty-three he had become head of his household, though it consisted at that time just of himself and his two sisters Sarah and Ann. It is likely that it was on one of his buying trips that he met his wife, Mary Ellen, who came from Lancashire, to settle for over thirty years in the Lindley area. Their cook had also been with them for this time, starting employment as a nurse to the family of four girls and finally a boy, Henry Stead Haigh. Mary the nurse eventually took over the running of the household. She also had moved away from her native Bedale in North Yorkshire to find work.

Sam was part of the family which owned David Haigh & Sons woollen merchants of St George's Street, Huddersfield. Others in the family lived locally in the Edgerton/Lindley area. Before fast transport, everyone lived fairly close to their place of business, even if they could afford to take a horse-drawn cab.

In later years Pond House would be used for Second World War refugees from the Channel Islands.

Croft House is long gone and a whole new estate of houses replaces it. But 100 years ago, the magnificent stone building was home to another Haigh family. Ben Haigh and his wife, Jane, had moved there in the mid to late nineteenth century. Ben was a woollen merchant, employing eleven men in his workshop. In addition, like many of his contemporaries, he employed another two men to work on his farm, supplying at least some of the wool. By 1900 his son Herbert had taken over the business and the house. Despite having no family at that time, he was wealthy enough to have two live-in servants – Annie the cook and Mabel a housemaid. Since his wife Kathleen and Mabel both came from Gloucester, it is probable that Mabel had been employed by Kathleen previously and had accompanied her mistress to the wilds of Yorkshire.

In a relatively close community the topics of conversation would have included the state of trade and the new factory legislation which imposed restricted hours. Factories were now only allowed to work on weekdays, and on Saturday mornings, starting at either 6 am and finishing at 11.30 am or 6.30 am to 12 noon. In both cases a further half hour was allowed for cleaning. The employers no doubt grumbled about this but the millhands would have enjoyed the extra half day off work.

Not all employers were factory owners. The Haggis family came from Halifax, where William had been a worsted spinner. Unemployed and unable to find work in the area, he, his wife Azubah and their nine children moved what was then a considerable distance to 27 Quarmby Fold. Here William became an overlooker in a mill, as well as farming in a small way for himself. With such a large family, there were plenty of hands to help, and the family prospered, despite having two more children. The farm provided employment

Figure 5. 27 Quarmby Fold, the farmhouse.

for two of the sons – Jabez who worked as a carter and William junior, who delivered milk. Again the girls went into the mills. William senior did not, unfortunately, live to enjoy a retirement but his widow continued to farm the area for many years before her son, who rejoiced in the name of Jabez Francis Oscar Haggis, took over. The house, built originally in 1840, looked out over the farm fields and had a large barn attached at the rear (Figures 5 & 6).

Figure 6. The barn at number 27, dated 1840.

Self-Employed

Not everyone hankered after the large workshop employing others nor did they inherit it. Some just wanted to work for themselves earning enough to keep their family, but without the pressure of being the Boss. Such were the two ladies who lived at numbers 7 and 9. Emma Shaw was a baker and confectioner, whilst next door was Hannah Kitson, whose husband John had died, leaving her to support herself through dressmaking. Perhaps she even made some of the clothes for the Stork family since her house backed on to theirs (Figure 6).

Though the Old Quarmby Hall has now been restored and is a lovely building, it gets little mention in many of the late nineteenth or early twentieth century records. It was simply referred to as number 49, where in 1901 Thomas Moore lived. His father, William, had been a woollen weaver in Lindley, but Thomas decided to branch out and become a coal dealer delivering coal to the local houses and shops. By 1902 Thomas had a growing family – Florence, James and George. The future would bring some sorrow as George was to be killed in the First World War when he was just eighteen (Figure 7).

Further along the Fold another self-employed man was Willie Booth, a greengrocer. His father, Joe William, had been a teamer, looking after and driving horses. Born in Stainland and originally living round on Quarmby Road they had moved into the Fold some years previously. His widow, Eliza, continued to live in their house with her two sons, Willie and Stanley. Willie had his own business, loading up with fresh fruit and vegetables each day and setting off with his horse and cart to take them round the neighbourhood to sell, a forerunner of today's supermarket delivery scheme. This sort of service was once a familiar sight in the villages. His house, store and stables have now been transformed into a modern house.

Round at number 59, we would have expected Samuel and Emma Johnson, who were both in their seventies, to be having a quiet retirement but with no social security available they continued working at their rug making trade. Living originally in Golcar, near

Figure 7. The war memorial.

where Emma had been born, they brought up their three sons and daughter, Sarah, whilst Samuel earned a living as a millhand. He had come over from Manchester to find work in the local mills before branching out in a small way for himself when he moved into the Fold.

Employees

By far the majority of the Quarmby Fold folk worked in the textile industry. All around were mills, mostly woollen or worsted and associated trades. Wellington Mills in Lindley was over fifty years old, whilst just down the road were the huge complexes of mills in Longwood, Milnsbridge and Marsh. A buzzer would sound in the morning to warn hands that they had better get a move on and not be late. More buzzers would sound for lunchtime and end of shift (Figure 8).

Whole families were employed in the same mills, many moving into the area because relatives were already there. These were the folk

Figure 8. Wellington Mills, Quarmby.

Figure 9. Numbers 15 and 17 (Henry Broadley lived at number 17).

who lived in the cottages.

Quarmby Fold is part way down a hill. A stream ran along what is now Greenfield Avenue, then through the Fold and on down Quarmby Clough, eventually draining into the River Colne. The spring water supplied many of the cottages via pipes but some had their own private well in the cellar of their house. They still contain water and have been known to flood at times.

At No. 61 was Tom Hoyle who was a woollen warp beamer. He and his wife Myra both came from the Holmfirth area but all their children were baptised in Lindley. Tom's younger brother Joe was to be found living round at No. 71. Who moved first? It is possible it was Joe, since his wife Edith originally came from Quarmby.

Others came from further afield to reap the benefits of factory work. Henry Broadley at No. 17 had come down from Leyburn in North Yorkshire to work as a woollen weaver. Not surprisingly the rest of his family, who were born in this area, eventually followed the same occupation (Figure 9).

Not everyone, though, came for textile work. Round at No. 11, John Moorhouse was a coachman. Many families in Huddersfield can trace their ancestry back in the same area for many generations but this family had moved down more than twenty years previously from Yarm near Durham. Like his father before him, the eldest son John worked with the horses as a groom but the rest of the family did go into the mills.

Another coachman lived in No. 33. Sam Kaye had been born in Hepworth, into a coal mining family, starting his working life down the mines. Becoming a coachman must have been healthier! He and his wife Sarah, who originally came from Snaith near Goole, had moved into the Fold with their daughter Blanche and three sons. They were another family who would personally be affected by the 1914-18 War when their son, Arthur Percy, was killed at the age of twenty-three, and was buried at Etaples in France.

Some people had totally different aspirations. Joe Ainley and his wife Harriet had moved from the Colne Valley some years previously. He worked in the chemical factories which were closely allied to the textile industry, providing the dyes needed for the cloth. However, their son, another Joe was more interested in cricket. He describes himself as a 'professional cricketer', and also played in the local Sunday League. Huddersfield's Cricket League had been formed to try to regulate cricket matches which were sometimes conducted under less than fair conditions – the winning team always seemed to be the one who provided the umpire! Many of the Yorkshire County players originally started in these local leagues though it does not appear that Joe Ainley was one.

Even in those days not everyone had a secure family life, though disruption was likely to be from death rather than divorce. Annie Whiteley had been widowed over forty years previously, since her husband John, an engineer, had died. Moving away from family and friends in Holmfirth where they had lived, she came to 15 Quarmby Fold. With a family of five children to bring up she must have had a hard life, since there were no social services or widow's pension. To make matter's worse, though most of her children eventually left home her eldest daughter, Emma, had also been left a widow at thirty with four small children. By 1901, the little cottage was crammed with the two widows and four grandchildren, all in their early twenties and all working in the local mills.

Life for women could be very difficult. Whilst not usually taking paid employment as a wife, as a widow it became a necessity unless the children were grown up and able to support their parent. In Quarmby Fold, besides Ann Whiteley, her daughter, Azubah Haggis and Hannah Kitson mentioned previously, there was Harriet Noble, who as a sixty-year-old widow was employed as a woollen burler, Elizabeth Varey whose daughter and son-in-law lived with her and helped to pay the bills, Eliza Hall who relied on a nephew as boarder, Eliza Booth a worsted mender, and Ada Shaw a woollen weaver. They all paid their rent and rates, were not a charge on the parish, but they were only allowed to vote in the local council elections and not in the parliamentary elections. Ada Shaw and Ann's daughter, Emma, did not even have a local vote!

Ada Shaw (she was really Leila Ada but presumably preferred the plainer 'Ada' to the posh 'Leila'), had been widowed at the comparatively young age of twenty-seven. Her husband Albert had been a millhand in Halifax where the family lived. Surprisingly all four children were baptised on the same day in 1894 – Sarah Elizabeth (known in 1901 as Lizzie), Ambrose, Tom and Ivy. Were the baptisms the result of a zealous vicar catching them all when asked to baptise the youngest or was Albert even then ill and wanting to baptise all his the children whilst he was alive to take part in the ceremony? Albert died just eighteen months later and the rest of the family subsequently moved to Quarmby Fold, where Ada took a job as a weaver to support her family. Her son Ambrose remained in Quarmby Fold, moving into another cottage in the 1920s.

Celebrations
Not all life was work however. Then, even more than now, royal events were the cause for celebrations and a day off work. After the deep mourning for Queen Victoria who had died at the beginning of 1901, the country was looking forward to enjoying the coronation of Edward VII. Everything had been prepared, bunting put up and events arranged for the summer, when the weather should have been (and in fact, was) at its best. Unfortunately, the King fell ill and had to undergo an operation causing the coronation to be postponed until later. Many of the villages went ahead with their celebrations in July anyway – after all, why waste a good feast? The corporation events waited until the official day in August. Then, as now, bands played in Greenhead Park, trees were planted in commemoration, fireworks were seen over Castle Hill.

The biggest difference would have been on the trams. Introduced in Huddersfield as horse-drawn vehicles in 1882, they had progressed to steam power, then electric. By 1901 they even ran on Sundays. For the coronation a magnificent spectacle would have been seen by the inhabitants of Quarmby Fold. On the Tuesday following the coronation, a tramcar illuminated by 1,200 lights of white, red, yellow, blue and green set off for Lindley. It was noted in the local paper that 'this number of lights will be three or four hundred more than in some other towns'. On one side the top outlined 'Long Live the King' and on the other 'God Bless the Queen', both emblazoned in electric lights. The tram even had curtains for the windows though the public were not allowed to actually ride on this particular tram. The *Examiner* newspaper stated that 'at the extreme ends of the car will be the device 'ER' and a five pointed star in lamps of various hues whilst flags etc. will be fixed on top of the car'. Even the trolley boom and handrails had lights on them. The tram left St George's Square at 8.30 at night going via Edgerton, Marsh and Lindley, then on to Outlane. The tram had been round the town centre and other outlying villages on other days.

People in the area came out to see the tram go past, though they could only enjoy extended pub opening hours on the day of the actual Coronation!

1902 would have been a year to enjoy in Quarmby. The Boer War had ended and young volunteers had arrived home. The new clock tower in Lindley was opened, new factory legislation reduced Saturday working hours, Yorkshire cricketers were one of the best sides ever, for the first time Empire Day had been celebrated on 24 May, and now a new King had begun a new reign. For a short time at least, Quarmby Fold folk must have looked forward to the future.

Glossary

Burler – cloth finisher
Draper's – shop selling cloth
Overlooker – supervisor in a mill
Teamer – driver of team of horses
Woollen – woven from short staple wool, giving fluffy finish
Worsted – long staple combed wool, giving smooth finish

Acknowledgements

The Quarmby Fold Folk - thanks to the residents who gave me such fascinating tales of the area. NB G Hall died in 1931. No current claimant to copyright is known.

Sources

Census records 1871, 1881, 1891, 1901
Parish records for Lindley, Holmfirth, Halifax, Huddersfield
Trade Directories: 1900, 1909, 1924
Ordnance Survey maps – 1854, 1893, 1907
Huddersfield Examiner, 1902
Huddersfield Examiner, obits 1948
Burgess Rolls 1899-1903
Huddersfield Cricket League records
West Yorkshire Archives – KC315

12. SIR THOMAS BROOKE

by John Goodchild

AN EMINENT WEST RIDING VICTORIAN, but a man now largely forgotten: Thomas Brooke, from 1899 Sir Thomas Brooke, baronet. When he died in 1908 Sir Thomas achieved obituary notices in *The Times* and the regional and local press, but a century later his name is largely meaningless in the very area in which in his time he took an active – indeed leading – role in so many disparate fields: in industry, in local affairs, in book and manuscript collecting. So who was Thomas Brooke, and why does he deserve some attention so long after his death?

The business from which Brooke derived his money and status and from which he was enabled to pursue his activities as a collector of considerable note, was that of John Brooke & Sons of Armitage Bridge, Huddersfield and London. It was of eighteenth century foundation and when it adopted limited liability in 1898 it had the then substantial capital of £200,000. In Brooke's later days, as woollen and fancy woollen cloth manufacturers, the firm had 200 looms at work. Brooke's own father, Thomas (of Northgate House, Honley) headed the business and fathered thirteen children, Thomas being the eldest of five sons, and was born in May 1830. He was educated privately before being sent to Cheltenham College and he became head of the family business upon his father's death in 1859, a position he held until 1879 when he retired – at nearly fifty years of age. Two of his younger brothers had been admitted to partnership in 1862. Brooke was, in his twenties, a vice-president of of the Huddersfield Chamber of Commerce, and subsequently served as its president. He was an able man of business and served from 1882 to his death as a director of the Great London and Western Railway Company, and also chaired the Equitable Life Assurance Society of the United States (as its London chairman), the Mutual Fire Insurance Corporation Ltd, the Palatinate Fire Insurance Corporation Ltd and the United Fire Re-insurance Co Ltd; and was vice-chairman of the Yorkshire Penny Bank and a director of other companies.

In non-remunerative public fields, Brooke had political ambitions. He was a Conservative and contested, unsuccessfully, the

Parliamentary borough of Huddersfield in 1874 and the new Colne Valley constituency in 1885, while a member of London's Carlton and Constitutional Clubs. Brooke was appointed a West Riding magistrate in 1864 and was active in that capacity in the days when the West Riding (outside the boroughs) was administered by the magistrates beyond a purely criminal jurisdiction. He sat on ten of the magistrates' committees, and again his abilities were recognised by his appointment as, first, vice-chairman and then in 1897 as chairman of the West Riding magistrates (shorn since 1889 of most of their administrative duties by the new West Riding County Council, of which he was a member too and indeed vice-chairman of that important regional parliament for some years) until he resigned in 1905. He held the honourable but largely inactive office of a West Riding Deputy Lieutenant, and in 1906 was made an Honorary Freeman of Huddersfield in recognition of his distinguished local public services.

Brooke joined the new and fashionable Huddersfield Volunteers in 1859 and rose in their ranks to become their Lt Col (as the 5th Administrative Battalion of the West Riding Rifle Volunteers) in 1866, retiring from that office in 1873. He was a family man too, living at Armitage Bridge House, built in 1820, and injured by the Holmfirth Flood of 1852. He married three times, but his only son died at the age of twenty. At Armitage Bridge a church had been erected in 1848 and a new parish created, and by the 1870s Brooke and the vicar of Almondbury were the patrons of that living. He was a strong supporter of the new Calder and Tributary Valleys Diocese of Wakefield. Later he was chairman of the building committee for the extension of the cathedral at Wakefield as a memorial to William Walshaw How, the first bishop of Wakefield.

Brooke, however, had a real personal interest in more academic matters. He was a founder member and treasurer of the Huddersfield Archaeological & Topographical Association of 1863, the direct precursor of the still flourishing Yorkshire Archaeological Society. He became its president in 1866, and continued to hold that office during a period of growth and influence on the part of that society until his death, forty-two years later. In this field he supported archaeological excavation, exhibitions and publications, expending £500 in having the Selby Abbey Chartulary in his own collection transcribed and published for the new Record Series, and presenting many volumes to the growing library of the YAS. His will provided for his manuscripts and books relating to Yorkshire to go to the YAS, where they are today for public use. He was also a vice-president of the records-publishing Surtees Society and was elected a Fellow of both the Society of Antiquaries of London (in 1871) and the Society of Arts. When the prestigious Yorkshire Geological Society held its annual meetings at Huddersfield in 1877, it was Thomas Brooke who presided.

In 1899 some national public recognition, at nearly seventy, came in the old Queen's birthday honours when Brooke was created a baronet – presumably endowing that distinction with his own monies, as was customary. No heir surviving him, the baronetcy became extinct at his death in 1908, but it was revived in a younger brother in 1919, and still exists.

Perhaps Brooke's greatest contribution to society was the collection of books and manuscripts which he made, described in his time as 'a remarkable collection of books which is conceded to be one of the finest libraries in England' and part of which (relating to Yorkshire) survives in total for public use today. Brooke records himself in the handsome, substantial and even opulent two-volumed catalogue of his own library which he published in 1891, that he had begun collecting in 1854, when in his mid-twenties. It is unfortunate that the surviving papers do not show how exactly he went about his collecting, apart from the fact that in part at least he bought heavily at book and MSS auctions; whether he haunted local booksellers' shops and local sales we do not know. He certainly bought heavily in local material at the early sales of the great bibliomaniac Sir Thomas Phillipps' from Middle Hall and later located in Thirlstaine House in Cheltenham; from the Phillipps Collection he purchased the papers of Ralph Thoresby the Leeds historian, of Joseph Hunter the historian of South Yorkshire; of Abraham Woodhead, the Fairfaxes, and so forth, which went at his death to form the bulk of the collections of Yorkshire source material at the YAS. A few of Brooke's catalogue of books for sale survive in the YAS Library, but from them it is quite impossible to deduce where his principal sources of books were. It seems likely that he was probably not quite the sufferer from bibliomania that were Sir Thomas Phillipps or even Brooke's fellow Yorkshireman, Edward Hailstone of Walton Hall near Wakefield – nor indeed as is the present writer. But Brooke served on the Council of the Bibliographical Society and was a member of the Henry Bradshaw Society, of the Early English Text Society and of the Roxburghe Club, all devoted to matters relating to book collecting.

In his lifetime Brooke had travelled extensively in Europe, in the United States and in Canada and India. But in his last years, he was dogged by ill health and even *The Times* records in the last few months of his life, in 1908, his illness on eight occasions; it records too, Brooke's death and his funeral, both in July 1908 when he was aged seventy-eight.

These were some of the many interests and activities of a great Yorkshire Victorian – a man significant locally in his own day, and whose beneficence and foresight in regard to his collection of Yorkshire material we have occasion to be thankful for in our own.

It may not come amiss, finally, to refer to a few other of the offices which Thomas Brooke held. For some twelve years he was a member of the South Crosland Local Board – the local authority of his own area – and for eight of those years its chairman. He served on the administrative body of the Yorkshire College and its successor, the University of Leeds; he had been president of the Huddersfield Mechanics' Institute and subsequently (to 1886) of the Huddersfield Technical College which it had promoted along with the Chamber of Commerce. He was a trustee of the local Almondbury Grammar School and a member of that select band, the local Commissioners of the Land and Income Taxes.

CONTRIBUTORS

THE EDITOR
7. 'THE FORGOTTEN PEOPLE OF HUDDERSFIELD':

Yorkshire's people and landscapes have always been material for the pen of the editor, **Stephen Wade,** who currently lectures in English at the University of Huddersfield. He has some family connections with the area, as one of his many uncles used to be landlord of *The Badger* in Fartown. Born in Leeds in 1948, Stephen lives in Lincolnshire but has relatives still in Yorkshire, and continues to write poetry and fiction with a West Riding setting. He has just completed a study of British regional writing (Greenwood Press), and his previous editing work has included *Gladsongs and Gatherings*, a collection of essays and memoirs about poetry in Liverpool. The article here reflects his continuing interests in immigrant communities in Yorkshire.

1. THE HUDDERSFIELD LUDDITE REBELLION OF 1812

John A Oldham was born at Clayton Heights, Bradford. He is married to Elaine, a schoolteacher. They have two children, Andrew and Amelia. He was educated at Buttershaw Comprehensive School, then studied printing at Leeds College of Technology and management at Leeds Polytechnic. He joined Waddingtons, the Monopoly and playing card manufacturers in Leeds, as a management trainee. After a spell with Yorkshire Television, he became Production Director of a publishing company, specialising in educational materials and short-run reprint books. He was subsequently appointed General Manager of Regent Print Ltd. That was closed in the early 1980s recession. He bought the goodwill of his old company with his redundancy money and is still in business today. He is Mentor for the Prince's Trust, and his published work include, *A History of Golcar, A Guided Walk Around Golcar* and a contribution to *Aspects of Huddersfield 1*, 'Legends of the Colne Valley'.

2. JAMES HIRST OF POLE MOOR: 'BOOK APRIL 24TH, 1836 - NOTABLE THINGS OF VARIOUS SUBJECTS IN DIARY FORM

Robert Gartery was born in Huddersfield and, until the age of seven, lived up Crimble Clough, not too far from James Hirst's cottage. His family moved across the valley to Linthwaite in 1954 and he went to Colne Valley High School in 1957. He studied mathematics and physics at the University of Newcastle upon Tyne, graduating in 1968. After taking a Diploma in Education, he taught mathematics in Derbyshire for four years. From 1973, he was firstly Head of Mathematics and then Senior Teacher at Nab Wood Grammar School in Bingley, where he and his wife brought up their two daughters. He is keenly interested in Genealogy and first became acquainted with James Hirst's diary when it was handed down to relations on his mother's side. His other interests include travel, theatre, walking and 'cooking candlelit dinners for my wonderful wife, Pam'.

3. THE CENTRE OF LIGHT AND KNOWLEDGE: THORNTON'S TEMPERANCE HOTEL 1854-1900

Alan J Brooke, a former miner at Emley Moor Colliery, studied Archaeology and Ancient History at Manchester University. He has written several pamphlets and articles on the working class history of the Huddersfield area, including *Liberty or Death*, co-authored with Lesley Kipling, an account of early nineteenth century Luddism and Radicalism. He is currently working on an illustrated record of the textile mills of Huddersfield and Vicinity *c.*1790-1914.

4. WOOL, WAR AND THE INDIES: THE FISHER LETTERS

Ian Sargen was born and brought up in Manchester, and then went to university in Liverpool and Cambridge. He returned to the north to teach English, first at Roundhay School, Leeds, and then at Rothwell Grammar School. He taught in three schools in Gloucestershire before becoming Head of a large 13-18 High School in East Anglia in 1981. His retirement in 1999 enabled him to find time at last to research the background to the Fisher letters, which had been lying in his desk drawer for forty years. He has enjoyed renewing his acquaintance with the life and history of the West Riding.

5. FILM-MAKING OVER THREE CENTURIES: JAMES BAMFORTH AND THE FILM MAKING PIONEERS

Ian Harlow is an exiled Yorkshireman, now living in Nottingham. He was born in Hull but was evacuated to Holmfirth during the war. He now has a cottage in the area and spends time exploring the snickets, ginnels and moors in the locality, as well as investigating local folk stories. He has retired after a lifetime as an accountant, having worked in this country and also spent four years in Africa. He is married with two children and two grandchildren whom he compels to walk the hills and listen to Grandad's tales of ancient Yorkshire.

6. READ HOLLIDAY AND LUNNCLOUGH HALL: A NINETEENTH CENTURY ENTREPRENEUR AND HIS HOME

David Griffiths is a senior manager with Kirklees Council, and has lived in Huddersfield since 1989. He was born and brought up in Rochdale, but lived and worked in London for many years before returning to the Pennines with his wife and two children. With degrees from St John's College, Cambridge and Birkbeck College, London, he has studied local history at the University of Bradford Centre for Continuing Education, and his contribution to this volume originated as a course assignment there.

8. HUDDERSFIELD PICTURE PALACES PRESENT 'QUEUEING FOR DREAMS'

Robert Preedy has lived in West Yorkshire for thirty years. His fascination with cinemas began when he worked as an usher in a local picture house. When he moved to Leeds he was surprised by the number of old cinemas still extant. In 1980 he published his first book, *Leeds Cinemas Remembered*. Since then he has written extensively about cinemas and theatres in Yorkshire. Roller Coasters also intrigued him and he published two pioneering books on this neglected subject. Not content with writing about cinemas, he ventured into the business in 1984 when he reopened the Castle Cinema, Pickering. This he ran for eight years before opening the Wetherby Film Theatre in 1994. Away from the big screen he has a parallel career in television and radio, working as a continuity announcer at Yorkshire Television and broadcasting a Saturday night Country music show on four stations including BBC Radio Leeds. His latest book is the history of the 1960s pop pirate off Scarborough, Radio 270. His next book looks at the story of James Corrigan and Batley Variety Club.

9. NURSES AND NURSING IN HUDDERSFIELD 1870-1960

Graham Thurgood started nursing in 1972 and worked in a variety of roles in hospital and as a district nurse. He has been involved in nurse education for a number of years since moving from Birmingham in 1989 when he came to work as a nurse tutor at the Huddersfield Royal Infirmary School of Nursing. Since 1997 he has been studying the history of nursing in Halifax and Huddersfield for a Ph.D research degree.
This is a two-part study using archival data and oral history interviewing. He created the West Yorkshire History of Nursing web site in December 2000. He works as a senior lecturer in the School of Human and Health Sciences, University of Huddersfield, where he created the West Yorkshire History of Nursing website in December 2000.

10. AN ARTISTS' COLONY IN LEEDS ROAD

Richard Stakes is a lecturer in education at Doncaster College and freelance writer specialising in the area of special needs. He is currently researching at Sheffield Hallam University. Main publications are (with Garry Hornsby), *Meeting Special Needs in Mainstream Schools* (David Fulton, 2nd edition, 2000) and *Change in Special Education* (Cassell, 1997). His familiarity with educational issues is surpassed by his encyclopaedic knowledge of British football.

11. QUARMBY FOLD FOLK

Vivien Teasdale was born in Hull, but has lived in the West Riding all her life, moving to Huddersfield in 1975. After training as a secretary and working in a variety of organisations, she began a teaching career which has spanned two decades, gaining a BA and MSc, along the way through part-time study. Although interested in all aspects of history, the impact of events on the 'ordinary folk' is of special importance. She is an experienced genealogist and has had a number of articles published in specialist magazines, as well as giving lectures on the subject.

12. SIR THOMAS BROOKE

John Goodchild, M Univ was born at Wakefield in 1935 and was involved in local history study from the age of about fifteen. He was founder-curator of Cusworth Hall Museum and spent his last years employed as Principal Local Studies Officer and Archivist at Wakefield, retiring at the age of fifty-nine. Subsequently, he has spent some seven years in establishing his own unique Local History Study Centre at Wakefield (which receives some 2,000 users a year and is available by appointment, free of charge), lecturing, writing and researching, and leading guided tours. He has now produced well over 150 books and printed essays. He continues actively to collect books, manuscripts, maps and illustrations relating principally to the central West Riding. John was awarded an Honorary Master's Degree by the Open University 'for academic and scholarly distinction, and for public services.' He has contributed essays to all the *Aspects* books on Barnsley, Wakefield, Rotherham, Leeds and Huddersfield.

Index - General

Index - People

Index - Places